MASOCHISM

A Jungian View

Lyn Cowan

MASOCHISM

A Jungian View

Spring Publications, Inc.
Dallas, Texas

© 1982 by Lyn Cowan. All rights reserved.
Fourth printing 1992
Published by Spring Publications, Inc.; P.O. Box 222069;
   Dallas, Texas 75222
Printed in the United States of America
Text printed on acidfree paper
Cover design by Kate Smith Passy

Library of Congress Cataloging in Publication Data

Cowan, Lyn, 1942–
      Masochism: a Jungian view.

      Includes bibliographical references.
      1. Masochism.   2. Sexual masochism.   3. Jung,
C. G. (Carl Gustav), 1875–1961.   I. Title.
RC553.M36C68 1982   155.2'32   82–16957
ISBN 0–88214–320–4

ACKNOWLEDGMENTS

Grateful acknowledgment is made to the following publishers for permission to use the material listed:

ATV Music Publishing of Canada Ltd. for lyrics from "Hit Me With Your Best Shot" by Eddie Schwartz; © 1980 by ATV Music Publishing.

American Broadcasting Companies, Inc., for excerpt from "Take the Money and Run" by Woody Allen.

Bear Brown Publishing Co. for lyrics from "Closer to the Ground" by Toni Brown; © by Toni Brown.

University of Chicago Press for excerpts from *The. Bacchae* by Euripides, translated by William Arrowsmith, in *Greek Tragedies*, Vol. 3; © 1959 by the University of Chicago Press.

Farrar, Straus & Giroux, Inc., for excerpt from *Of Love and Lust: On the Psychoanalysis of Romantic and Sexual Emotions* by Theodor Reik; © 1957 by Theodor Reik.

Field Newspaper Syndicate for excerpt from Ann Landers's column, appearing in the *Minneapolis Tribune*, 25 May 1980; © 1980 by Field Newspaper Syndicate.

Macmillan Publishing Co., Inc. and Macmillan Press Ltd. for excerpt from *Sparkenbroke* by Charles Morgan; © 1936 by Charles Morgan.

For Pat, Jim, Chris, John, and Valerie,
who all helped congeal the madness.

The art of our necessities is strange,
That can make vile things precious.
SHAKESPEARE, *King Lear*

CONTENTS

A Confessional Fantasy...

To write on a subject such as this is to fall headlong into a masochistic venture. I have a profound aversion to it and an equally profound fascination, rebelling even while my soul rushes into it. I am, classically, in bondage to my theme. All the symptoms and fetishes are activated; the page becomes a canvas on which to paint tortured images to rival Bosch, and the images flay and flagellate me. Defeated before the end of the first paragraph, I start with a negative, a descent, and there is no telling where the bottom is.

I am aware that much of my own psychology emerges, exhibiting itself here and there between periods and paragraphs, exposing itself behind adjectives. This cannot be helped and ought not to be avoided. It is part of masochism—confession, exposure, revealing, stripping, reducing to essentials. Masochism is essential, less for sexual pleasure than for the very life of the soul. We may have to apply the whip occasionally to get on with it, but once the binding power of the fantasy takes effect, there is no going back. The fantasy cannot be stopped, and it goes on creating reality.

Masochism, before it is anything else, is essential reality. It is not a mere perversion, not a distortion or deviation, but essence: a reflection of the soul in its tortured, most inarticulate moments. These are moments of exquisite pain, imminent death, intolerable images, of unbearable passion that ignites both body and soul. This book is indeed a "strange necessity."

*

I owe an unpayable debt to Mary Lynn Kittelson, word-worker extraordinaire, who in editing the manuscript suffered most of this work with me and who became godmother to it when her loyal hand was most needed. She enriched this book by her imaginative insight, craftsmanship in writing, criticism, and unflogging devotion to the project. Amongst the many other individuals who contributed to and influenced this book, a special few command special thanks: Caroline Weening, editor, who saw something redeemable in the midst of my chaotic manuscript and, wielding a magic lead pencil, called it forth; to Judy Gray-Schafman for provoking me to start at all; to Mary Fiedler, who had faith from the beginning; to the late Jeanne Pearce, Doug Belknap and Demos Lorandos for reading early pieces of draft and responding with equally passionate measures of encouragement and criticism; to analysands who granted me the privilege of entering their private agonies and ecstasies and who gave permission to include their dreams and fantasies in this book; and especially to Pat Berry, Jim Hillman, Chris Santella, John Pearce, and Valerie Lopez, who, over the years, have given me more than they know in ways they cannot imagine.

Wherever the book fails, I am there alone.

An Opening

Masochism . . . Strange smiles play on people's lips at the mention of the word. The grunts of disapproval seem to echo with smacks of embarrassed appetite. The grimaces of disgust may also be upside-down smiles of anticipation in disguise. What lies at the heart of this approach/avoidance to masochism? What makes it so important as to gain so much, and such contradictory, attention?

The range of experiences that may fall under the heading of "masochism" is enormous, from the pleasure/pain of overt sexual activity of the leather-and-chains set to the covert emotional hurts that we attract almost daily, ones which bring some sense of satisfaction. In the broadest use of the word, masochists include not only the bondage-and-discipline enthusiasts, but also those who get into and stay in relationships and situations and attitudes which bring them pain and no apparent pleasures, those who don't know when to quit. Jealous lovers, jilted lovers, the sexually liberated and the sexually dependent—all have their masochistic moments. Everywhere we find harried executives, neglected spouses, unappreciated activists who feel themselves, somewhere, to be abused.

Masochism need not be bloody and blatant to make its presence felt. There is that very sizable segment of humanity—that classical locus of the norm, the Middle. We in the Middle go to work every day, bearing up stoically under pressures of incompetent management, inflation, taxes, boredom and computer breakdowns. We in the Middle, truth to tell, have peculiar, shameful, sexual, masochistic fantasies which are not usually acted upon in bed. Here in the Middle also dwell those of us who cherish secret but modest ambitions, plans, hopes which somehow never become realities, which turn instead to painful memories and bitter disappointments.

Masochism has always been thought of as an extreme. Masochists have been thought to live in extremity, on the fringe. The segregationist in each of us is offended at the inclusion of kinky Masochist within the straight Middle. We imagine the masochist, as we do criminals and the mentally retarded, to belong only on the fringe, in that nebulous realm called psychopathology.

It is not hard to understand how we have come to accept this placement. Krafft-Ebing, the nineteenth-century psychiatrist who coined the term, subsumed masochism under the broad heading of "General Pathology" in his famous volume, *Psychopathia Sexualis*, in 1876. Newly designated and classified, masochism became a pathological, sexual, and psychopathic phenomenon all at once. A bit later, Freud considered masochism under the rubric of "perversion," keeping it still in the ghetto of abnormality. Other twentieth-century students of masochism have dealt with it under labels of "character disorder," "neurosis," "the masochistic personality," and as a form of "obsessive-compulsive neurosis." It is now listed in the American Psychiatric Association's *Diagnostic and Statistical Manual* (DSM–III) under "Psychosexual disorders," subheading "Paraphilias," code 302.83, "sexual masochism."

Lately, Ann Landers managed, as usual, to condense this popular attitude in her response to this letter:

> Dear Ann: I am a married woman in my early 40s who needs your opinion on our life style. My husband and I are into dominance. I don't mean beating up on each other or anything brutal, but we do a lot of hard spanking on bare derrieres, which is a terrific turn-on before love-making. We are told dominance is very big in England.
>
> It all began when we joined this club in Westchester, N.Y. There are five other couples. We meet once a week (in our homes) and do our thing.

Recently we began switching partners, and this has added a lot of excitement to the get-togethers. Variety *is* the spice of life. To add a little zing to our love-making, Harry bought me a riding crop for Valentine's Day. He has used it on me a few times, and I'll admit it hurts, but it does rev me up a lot—and I don't mind. Both Harry and I have been reading your column since we were teenagers, and we respect your opinion. We would like to know if you approve of what we are doing. (Signed: New York Question)

Ann Says: You don't need my approval. If you and Harry want to blister each other's behinds with whips, it's nobody else's business. But I feel I should tell you that people who go in for group sex and inflicting pain to hype the excitement of love-making are sick, sick, sick. Dominance (also known as bondage) is not new. It has been a part of the kinky scene for centuries.[1]

"Sick, sick, sick," says Ann—just as we thought all along. From the moral point of view, which sees things in terms of right and wrong, and the medical point of view, which sees things in terms of sickness and health, and the social point of view, which sees things in terms of redeeming social value or lack thereof, masochism falls on the minus side every time. Collectively, it is held to be morally wrong, medically sick, and socially destructive.

However, this book is psychological and works within a model of *understanding* masochism, its import and meaning for psyche. To understand is to stand under, to go below the surface, and thus the direction of movement is downward rather than distant, a direction of depth. We will neither condemn nor treat masochism, nor seek social approval, but try rather to discern what psychological purposes it may serve.

*

A psychological approach implies many things, so some comments on premises, vocabulary, and method are in order.

My usage of the word "psyche" is, in most cases, close to the original Greek meaning, "soul." When the Greek word *logos* ("word," "speech," "meaning") is coupled with *psyche*, we have both an important word usage, *psychology*, and a first premise, that "soul" has meaning and is articulate. "Psychology," then, evokes soul and all we associate with it: subjectivity, experience, emotion, reflection, and a religious concern for values and meaning. Psychology is not just another adjunct to other sciences, such as physiology, chemistry, medicine, etc. I follow C. G. Jung in the conviction that psyche is a "first principle" itself. While psyche is shaped by other fields of study, it is not dependent on them for its existence or definition. In short, psyche is not derived from anything else, not reducible to anything else. It may be thought of as both *that which* we study and *that perspective through which* we study. As a collective and individual phenomenon, psyche is both a standpoint from which we see experiences objectively and the 'place' in which we experience subjectively.

The word "soul" evokes that religious sense and concern for the meaning of events and value of experiences, and for this reason I prefer it to "psyche." I do not attach any creedal or dogmatic associations to either "religion" or "soul." "Religion," or "the religious attitude," is to be understood in Jung's broad sense, as

> a careful consideration and observation of certain dynamic factors that are conceived as "powers": spirits, daemons, gods, laws, ideas, ideals, or whatever name man has given to such factors in his world as he has found powerful, dangerous, or helpful enough to be taken into careful consideration, or grand, beautiful, and meaningful enough to be devoutly worshipped and loved.[2]

Soul can be imagined as a metaphorical 'place' where religious experience happens, or where religion is experienced. It is more than this, of course; yet the more one tries to define soul, the more elusive it becomes.

Though I cannot identify soul with anything else, I also can never grasp it by itself apart from other things, perhaps because it is like a reflection in a flowing mirror, or like the moon which mediates only borrowed light. But just this peculiar and paradoxical intervening variable gives one the sense of having or being a soul. However intangible and indefinable it is, soul carries highest importance in hierarchies of human values, frequently being identified with the principle of life and even of divinity.[3]

The terms "fantasy," "image," "imagination," and "reality" as used in this book imply a second premise: while soul or psyche *receives* impressions and experiences, it also *creates* them. Jung says that "the psyche creates reality every day."[4] He speaks of "fantasy" as "imaginative activity," calling it "the direct expression of psychic life, of psychic energy which cannot appear in consciousness except in the form of images or contents. . . ."[5] Jung not only reaffirms psyche as the source of inner reality (as opposed, say, to the material reality of the body or the logical reality of the mind), but also reaffirms the serious import of our fantasies as statements of inner reality which do not always depend on an external referent for their substance or meaning. His definition recognizes the importance and dignity in fantasy and image-making; they emerge as natural, primary expressions of psyche, giving us a basis of psychic *reality.*

This approach carries important implications for our understanding of psychopathology. "Psychopathology" is not simply synonymous with "sickness" in the medical sense nor "sin" in the religious sense. Both obscure our vision with respect to what psyche might be *saying* in its pathology. Both refuse to recognize that pathologizing is one of the soul's characteristic activities. Fortunately, the fact that we use the term "psychopathology" suggests that somewhere we still recognize its original meaning in Greek: the meaning *(logos)* of suffering *(pathos)* of the soul *(psyche)*. James Hillman has turned this deftly to the "the soul's suffering of meaning.''[6] Through its ''psychopathologies,'' the soul speaks of its conditions, and perhaps its intentions, by means of symptoms, dreams, fantasies, and behavior; it does so individually and collectively.

Jung's pregnant comment that ''image is psyche''[7] is a third major premise. It elevates ''image'' from a residual thing, an afterimage or leftover *(Tagesrest)*, an object of sensate or material perception (through the actual eyes), to an experience of inner reality (through the imaginal eyes). The psychological mode of looking at things (persons, objects, ideas) is really a looking *through* things. In order to 'see' psychologically, we have to look ''away from the natural reality of the perceptual toward the psychic reality of the imaginal.''[8] Apparent seeing becomes transparent seeing. Most importantly, since image is psyche and image is never literal, what is imaginally perceived can be truly expressed or described only in the language of metaphor, of likenesses. This procedure resembles more closely the writing of a poem or the painting of a picture than the block-like categories and conceptualizations of scientific textbooks.

Thus this is not a 'scientific' study of masochism, since objectivity is just as questionable, and just as legitimate, as subjectivity. This is both my fourth premise and my methodology. As we proceed by amplifying, unfolding, circling around, zooming in close to focus sharply and then fading out, we realize that science is not the only model of investigation, and not even the best. My loose-jointed method is not so much to instruct and explain as to evoke and describe. Masochism is a paradoxical, emotionally-laden, scientifically-named, historically-conditioned psychic fantasy. Because it appears in a multiplicity of images, a multiplicity of meanings is attached and we require a multiplicity of approaches to understand it. The models used in this book—myth, religion, alchemy, history—embody most fully, in their language and imagery and very nature, the deep roots of psychic life: what Jung called ''archetypes.''[9]

The archetypal realm, the place of original imprinting (Greek *ar-che*, "first," and *typos*, "mold" or "pattern"), is the mythic realm, the place of original experience. Myth is not a by-product afterthought, or pale reflection of social patterns—myth-making is a spontaneous, primary activity of psyche. Nor is myth only a 'projection' of psychic figures, for this makes myth secondary, presupposing a projector. Mythic events and persons, like Dionysus in Chapter 6, are experiences of psyche. Without being literal, myths are 'true' stories and 'real' persons in that they are psychologically true and real. Myth makes psyche intelligible. Nor Hall captures this sense of myth when she writes,

> This urge to express what [is] seen and heard beneath the surface of ordinary reality requires a "language of the soul" and is one of the ways mythology comes into being. Putting the events of the extraordinary experience together in a meaningful way makes a *muthos*, a myth—not a made-up story but literally a "mouthing," a telling of primary experience using the first words of coming to consciousness. . . . Myth is the original mother tongue.[10]

Thus myth is a matrix to which we revert for the sense of depth and meaning.

One last word about 'methodology': our journey has boundaries. I have not struck off around the globe to do cultural comparisons but have remained within the history and traditions of Western civilization. I have not climbed mountains of statistics on sexual deviance nor crossed oceans of detailed case histories. The material in this book has come from various sources—psychiatry, religion, literature, mythology, patients, myself—and my method has been to spin the material out, like the Fates who appear in later chapters. Then, I have woven these various threads to make a textured book rather than a textbook. This is a method of collecting and piecing together what seems to fit, not unlike a scrapbook whose fragments are yet all of a piece. And it is a method of amplification, to increase the volume and resonance of a dream, an experience, an idea, an image, and to enlarge its context. Indeed amplification helps create a context. It seeks to clarify by description rather than by definition. To use a different metaphor, it emphasizes tone, shading, and subtle ambiguity rather than sharp distinctive lines and balanced composition. The material determines the method, as the image teaches technique.

Enter Dionysus. He is of soft, even effeminate, appearance. His face is beardless; he is dressed in a fawn-skin and carries a thyrsus (i.e., a stalk of fennel tipped with ivy leaves). On his head he wears a wreath of ivy, and his long blond curls ripple down over his shoulders.

Throughout the play he wears a smiling mask.

The Bacchae: Opening scene

CHAPTER 1

The Possibilities of Perversion

Pentheus: You say you saw the god.
What form did he assume?

Dionysus: Whatever form he wished.
The choice was his, not mine.
EURIPIDES, *The Bacchae*

Of course sex is dirty if it's done right.
WOODY ALLEN, "Take the Money and Run"

Since the word was first invented more than a century ago, masochism has had very bad press; we never think of masochism as genuine suffering, but only as fraudulent, self-inflicted pain. In our time, suffering in any brand or size looks somehow suspect or stupid or sick. This book approaches masochism in two important ways: on one side, it searches out value in masochism, to help redeem it from the hell of meaninglessness. On the other side, it seeks for ways in which masochism may become so dominant that it blocks passages to deeper psychological recognitions which make for individuality, for what Jung has called "the individuation process."[1]

Like the phenomenon it describes, the term "masochism" is in a state of constant abuse, of persistent, paradoxical wrongness. It is already an overloaded word, carrying too many associations and connotations. Yet it carries also too few. The way we use it, "masochism" refers only to one side of the experience, the negative, the sick side. But precisely because the word is so weighted with emotion, affect, image, and history, we cannot afford to abandon it. If we change it, we lose some of the weight and pathology it carries—the sense of weakness and inferiority and shame it implies. It is a loaded word and we need the word to carry the load.

The essence of masochism is psychological. This is to say that masochism is primarily metaphorical, a likeness. Masochism has been studied for the last hundred years as a sexual aberration or perversion, as a neurotic character formation ("moral masochism"), and as a peculiar component in some types of religious experience. But what we call sexual masochism, moral masochism, religious masochism are all metaphors through which psyche speaks of its suffering and passion. They are containers, backdrops, or contexts from which to reflect upon the psychology of masochism.

There is no *single* understanding of masochism, even when we experience it as single individuals in specific instances. As a metaphor, masochism does not lend itself to a fixed definition; as a psychological experience, it is essentially paradoxical. Every psychic image is ambiguous in content and ambivalent in value;[2] as an archetypal phenomenon, masochism is one of the ways the depth of psychic life is experienced. Rooted in the imagination, it expresses itself in metaphors, likenesses of ways the soul loves and suffers.

*

People have been fascinated and repelled by their own and others' sufferings for as long as we know. For centuries, the experience of simultaneous suffering and pleasure was understood through contexts other than the particular field which came to be known as psychology—contexts such as myth, alchemy, romantic love, and religion. It was only in 1876 that Richard von Krafft-Ebing published *Psychopathia Sexualis*, introducing the term "masochism" into the language. Naming it and placing it under the heading of "General Pathology" changed it, and masochism acquired a new context of scientistic medical psychology.

Krafft-Ebing regarded masochism as a primarily sexual phenomenon, making the sexual instinct his starting point for an anatomy of its psychology. This is his definition of masochism:

> By masochism I understand a peculiar perversion of the psychical sexual life in which the individual affected, in sexual feeling and thought, is controlled by the idea of being completely and unconditionally subject to the will of a person of the opposite sex; of being treated by this person as a master, humiliated and abused. This idea is colored by lustful feeling; the masochist lives in fantasies, in which he creates situations of this kind and often attempts to realize them. By this perversion his sexual instinct is often made more or less insensible to the normal charms of the opposite sex—incapable of a normal sexual life—psychically impotent.[3]

According to Krafft-Ebing, the distinguishing characteristic of masochism is *subjection* to another person, an idea which rules the psychosexual fantasy life of the masochist. He proceeds further, stating that masochism is a pathological growth of specific *feminine* psychical characteristics, the "determining marks" of which are "suffering, subjection to the will of others, and to force";[4] and finally, masochism is a "congenital sexual perversion" and an "original abnormality,"[5] resulting in and from "psychical impotence." So it was that "masochism" came to designate a psychopathology of sexuality. So it was too that our view of the "masochistic" experience lost its sense of the soul's suffering and its intrinsically metaphorical speech.

By avoiding a literal reading, and by listening for the metaphors in Krafft-Ebing, we can hear psyche giving us a *logos* (a "logic," a "meaning," and a "speech") of masochism in psychosexuality ("images of sexuality"). We will return again and again, with pleasure and pain, to the ideas of "perversion," "sex," "subjection," "humiliation," "lustful feeling," and "psychical impotence," trying to hear the metaphorical resonances in them, trying to deepen their significances by restoring their polyvalent imaginal aspects.

Let us look through this medical and scientific surface to the assumptions and to the imaginal figures behind—and below—Krafft-Ebing's ideas. On the surface, investigation took on the qualities of its patron God, Apollo: cool, academic, enlightened. Krafft-Ebing's great work shines with brilliance—and with an inclination to kill, with well-aimed, sharp, arrow-like insights, from an emotional distance. The Apollonic viewpoint, because it requires light and clarity and objectivity, relegated masochism to darkness and shrouded it in a pall of pathology. There its ambiguity appeared as perversion, and its subjectivity made it a subject to be observed objectively.

We can observe this same Apollonic distance and sharpness in this statement by Krafft-Ebing: "We are certainly far beyond sodomitic idolatry, the public life, legislation and religious exercises of ancient Greece, not to speak of the worship of Phallus and Priapus, in vogue among the Athenians and Babylonians, or the Bacchanalian feasts of the Romans. . . ."[6]

In the monotheistic, Christianized imagination of the nineteenth century, the 'normal' manifestation (note the singular) of sexuality excluded all the priapian monstrosities which belonged to an earlier pagan imagination. But as Freud told us only a few decades after Krafft-Ebing's work, the return of the repressed is inevitable. The return of Priapus with his oversized phallus is announced on every page of *Psychopathia Sexualis*. Thinking we have gone beyond him, we meet his freakish sexuality everywhere, in Krafft-Ebing's categories of masochism, sadism, fetishism, onanism, homosexuality, etc. Priapus is present—erect and tall—in Krafft-Ebing's, and our, uprightness and in the inescapability of sexual feelings, especially the freaky ones.

Actually, to begin a study of masochism with the sexual instinct is already an acknowledgment of the god Priapus and his potency. Krafft-Ebing's work on masochism is a study of sexuality manifesting itself beyond the normal, in the realm of Priapus, who was so ugly that his own mother, Aphrodite, rejected him. It is the place where sex is distorted, perverted, inverted, and where the god of the giant phallus is both cause of and cure for impotence. Priapus's outrageous and outsized genital anatomy is a seminal figure in Krafft-Ebing's work, informing sexual psychopathy from the shadows.

Krafft-Ebing was an expert on masochism; Masoch was a case of it. The style in which each man approached his subject is instructive: the physician Krafft-Ebing gave us definitions of masochism; the writer Masoch gave us images, as in

> . . . a large oil painting. . . . A beautiful woman, naked beneath her dark furs, was resting on an ottoman, supported on her left arm. A playful smile hovered on her lips and her thick hair was tied in a Grecian knot and dusted with snow-white powder. Her right hand played with a whip while her bare foot rested nonchalantly on a man who lay on the ground before her like a slave, like a dog. The pronounced but well-shaped features of the man showed quiet melancholy and helpless passion; he gazed up at her with the fanatical, burning eyes of a martyr.[7]

In this passage, 'perversion' is seen in a painting, 'masochism' cast in an art form. Here, a naked woman in furs, resting, with a whip—'masochism' is evoking not a stereotypical sadist but a seductive, powerful goddess. Here, the 'masochist' appears as worshipper and slave, wholly absorbed in and focused on this Greek-like divinity, where ''helpless passion'' has not yet been reduced to ''psychical impotence,'' nor melancholic devotion to sexual ''subjection.''

In his pioneering work and sympathetic attitude, Krafft-Ebing was ahead of his time, while in another sense Masoch was far behind it, a pagan Greek at heart. The cool sexuality and moral rectitude that characterized the Victorian era, the bracing and upright climate of Northern Europe,[8] were intolerable to Masoch. His goddess of love, Venus, she of the southern, warm, erotic clime, tells the main character,

> . . . you nurse a secret craving for a life of sheer paganism. You modern men, you children of reason, cannot begin to appreciate love as pure bliss and divine serenity; indeed, this kind of love is disastrous for men like you, for as soon as you try to be natural you become vulgar. To you Nature is an enemy. You have made devils of the smiling gods of Greece and you have turned me into a creature of evil. You may cast anathemas on me, curse me or offer yourself in sacrifice like frenzied bacchantes at my altar, but if one of you so much as dares to kiss my crimson lips, he must make a barefoot pilgrimage to Rome in sackcloth and ashes, and pray until the cursed staff grows green again, while all around me roses, violets, and myrtle bloom everlastingly. Their fragrance is not for you. Stay in your northern mists and Christian incense and leave your pagan world to rest under lava and the rubble. Do not dig us up; Pompeii was not built for you, nor were our villas, our baths and our temples. You do not need the gods—they would freeze to death in your climate![9]

No wonder Leopold von Sacher-Masoch reacted instinctively in protest against it when his contemporary, Krafft-Ebing, turned his upper-case name into a lower-case noun to describe a sexual pathology. We can imagine that Masoch felt a deep betrayal: from the author's viewpoint, Krafft-Ebing—and now the world—had misunderstood and misused his writings. The passion and desire—now called "masochism"—that informed and inflamed his social philosophy was to be eliminated, and the peculiarity of his aesthetic sensuality was coldly scrutinized—and then regretted—as a sexual anomaly.

One place we find a similar conflict now is on the 'shadier' streets of our cities and towns. Newspapers regularly report that pornography is fighting the guardians of moral and property values for some territory in our neighborhoods. Pornography delights in freakish, lusty sex, in exotic sexual partners and positions, tantalizing environments, all sorts of taboo-breaking, and especially in sadomasochistic sex. Perhaps it is here in pornography's storefront displays that we might find altars to Masoch's Venus, although she has, as we might expect, lost much dignity in her translation to human proportions.

The clean strength of quiet Victorian sex can look just as monstrous and freakish as the perverted, loud lust of pagan sex. Advocates of pornography, whether they watch smugly from behind corners, make 'intellectual' statements within the safety of their homes, or openly rally, regard pornography's enemies as uptight, narrow, repressed, wilted on the vine, cold to sexual variety and honest lust. This same controversy and confusion is reflected in our society's endless proliferation of sexual manuals—solid American know-how and a clean technological approach to wiping out sexual problems.

Unfortunately, pornography and sex manuals lack a connection with psyche, religion, art—that vital relationship with soul. We cannot remain in Krafft-Ebing's fantasy of scientism, nor in the sterile approaches and stand-offs of modern times. There is godliness, in spite of so much cleanliness, and there are many gods, many different visions of the phenomenon we call "masochism." Without them, we are blind to the complexities and meanings of the experience. Without Eros, for example, we miss the erotic love in masochism which moves Psyche; we see only 'lustful feelings.' Without Hermes, we miss the ambiguities, the hidden hermetic meanings, and the stolen moments of deliciously deviant, borderline sex; we see only a 'peculiar perversion.' Without Dionysus, we miss the religious purpose in perversion, the rapturous delight in submission, the worship in wild abandon, the deliverance from the bondage of normalcy; we see only 'subjection' and 'impotence.'

*

In moving from Krafft-Ebing to Freud, our focus shifts. It has become practically a dogma of psychoanalytic thought that masochism is a sexual condition in which punishment is required before satisfaction can be reached. Freud understood the phenomenon as resulting from an "unconscious feeling of guilt" as "a need for punishment by some parental authority," a sexualization of morality and regression from morality back to the Oedipus-complex. The masochism creates a "temptation to 'sinful acts' which must then be expiated by the reproaches of the sadistic conscience . . . or by chastisement from the great parental authority of Fate."[10] In brief, the sadistic super-ego must be bought or bribed; punishment is the payment, satisfaction is the reward.

Writing in 1919, Freud found the genesis and reference point for masochism in the Oedipus-complex. Masochism, he said, actually begins in a pre-masochistic phase of infantile sexuality, when the wish for the incestuous object-choice (father or mother) must be repressed. Guilt enters at this point, of unknown origin but connected with incestuous wishes and justified by the persistence of those wishes in the unconscious. The parent figure then becomes the dispenser of punishment instead of love and appears in fantasies of beating, spanking, etc. But guilt is not the whole content of masochism; Freud said the love-impulse figures also. The fantasy of being beaten becomes the meeting place between the sense of guilt and sexual love. "It is not only the punishment for the forbidden genital relation, but also the regressive substitute for it."[11]

So punishment-reward in a progression does not fully describe the masochistic experience. As Freud perceived, the pain or suffering *is* already the reward or gratification, not only a preliminary to it: "The suffering that the neurosis involves is the very element which makes it of value to the masochistic trend." Even when one form of suffering gives way to another, what matters is that "a certain level of suffering should be maintained."[12]

In sexual terms, then, gratification need not be limited to the moment of orgasm; it begins with the punishment, in the excitement and arousal of both genitals and fantasy. Whether it involves literal pain or not, the punishment desired by the masochist is enjoyed in and of itself. Punishment and satisfaction both give pleasure—and humiliation. The masochistic moment may feel like a psychic orgasm, a violent and ecstatic loss of control. Usually the masochistic moment is longer—minutes or hours or even days. It is that span of time in which we somehow do not turn away from our pain; indeed, we almost desire it to embrace us, even though we cannot bear it. When masochism has become a center of one's meaning—a "core complex"—the masochistic moment may be said to last a lifetime.

Freud was more obvious than Krafft-Ebing in his connection with the gods. He used myth and its language to articulate his psychology. Oedipus, Thanatos, Eros, Fate—these figures populate and give substance to his psychological ideas. The power of the mythic deities and the inadequacy of a single referent (Oedipus) in understanding masochism is admitted in Freud's comment: "For the moment we must bow to those superior forces [the instincts of Eros and Death] which foil our efforts. Even to exert a psychical influence upon a simple case of masochism is a severe tax on our powers."[13] Later we will see other mythic persons—Dionysus, Prometheus, Saturn, et al.—as giving substance to our psychological ideas of masochism. For now, let us look at the relationship between religion and masochism from a more familiar context—Christianity.

Before science regarded masochism as a disease, religion regarded it as a cure. The medieval Church considered the sacrament of Penance part of its general ministry for the "cure of souls." So it was and is the soul that is 'diseased' and in need of 'cure.' The language of the early Christian Penitentials[14] is medical language, though inflected with a spiritual rather than a biological resonance. Penance is a "remedy" and "medicine for sin." Like those early Greek and Roman physicians who did not perceive science and religion as conflicting disciplines, medieval priests saw the Penitentials as medicinal prescriptions for soul-diseases. The penitent

> was regarded as one morally diseased and ill, and his treatment is, in the Penitentials, repeatedly, even habitually, referred to as the task of the moral physician. His sins are the symptoms of disease. The penalties enforced are 'medicaments,' 'remedia'—measures designed to restore his moral and spiritual health.[15]

The root of the word "penance" means punishment ("penalty," "penal," "punish" are all related). As we know, Freud and modern psychology have made much of the concept of masochism as a need for punishment. From the religious perspective, the desire to be beaten, whipped, and punished expresses the desire for 'penance.' This desire is not to be taken lightly, nor profaned by personalistic causal explanations. Psychiatric terms, and even psychoanalytic theory, do not do justice to this desire, which is essentially religious, rather than symptomatic of personal pathology.

St. Teresa of Avila wrote that "when these longings to serve Him come upon me, I want to do penance, but am not [physically] able. Penance would be a great relief to me, and is in fact a relief and a joy."[16] From the religious standpoint, to seek penance—which entails humiliation, shame, and perhaps pain—is a move toward health. It is motivated by a desire for health (salus in Latin, from which the word "salvation" derives). In fact to deny one's need of the 'medicine' of penance used to be seen as 'sick,' i.e., morally deficient. The humiliation of penance (criticism, punishment, repentance) adds to the good things of life (joy, pleasure, glory, praise) and thus provides a way in which one can be made fully human and restored to health. The desire to be punished, or to do penance, can be seen either as a means of finding sexual satisfaction or spiritual satisfaction, or both. Either way, there is pleasure in it.

The medieval Flagellants provide an extreme and public rendition of the wildly erotic pain and pleasure of religious and masochistic impulses. In the early eleventh century, monastic hermits of Camaldoli and Fonte Avellana in Italy took up the practice of self-flagellation as a form of penance. It became a regular feature of monastic life, soon fleeing the seclusion of the monasteries to become the most common of all penitential techniques. In fact, the term *disciplina*, once used to describe all manner of penances authorized by the Church, came to be restricted to mean "scourge."

At first it may be hard for us to imagine what bloody passion drove these Flagellants, what frenzied desire could reach consummation only in torn flesh and self-degradation. We are accustomed to subtler, vaguer, and more interior pleasure/pain. It seems shockingly excessive—yet fascinating—to read the experience of the fourteenth-century monk who, on a cold winter night,

> shut himself up in his cell and stripped himself naked . . . and took his scourge with the sharp spikes, and beat himself on the body and on the arms and on the legs, till blood poured off him as from a man who has been cupped. One of the spikes on the scourge was bent crooked, like a hook, and whatever flesh it caught it tore off. He beat himself so hard that the scourge broke into three bits and the points flew against the wall. He stood there bleeding and gazed at himself. It was such a wretched sight that he was reminded in many ways of the appearance of the beloved Christ, when he was fearfully beaten. Out of pity for himself he began to weep bitterly. And he knelt down, naked and covered in blood, in the frosty air, and prayed to God to wipe out his sins from before his gentle eyes.[17]

The Flagellants marched from one town to the next, in procession, picking up new penitents as they passed through. Sometimes numbering in the thousands, they would march to a church, form a circle in front of it, and perform a highly ritualized penitential ceremony. Stripped to the waist, the penitents would proceed through chants and hymns, prostrating themselves in contrition, rising again to sing hymns. The ritual finally culminated in a severe flagellation of all the participants, sometimes lasting for hours. At the end, these gaunt figures, faces pressed to earth in shame and rapture, their backs beaten to raw meat, their whips dyed blood-red, were yet lifted into ecstasy. The emotional intensity and searing vision of this large-scale public penance never failed to win still more converts to the movement.

Rules for members of Flagellant groups were precise and iron-clad; all had to swear obedience to the Master of the group, but only for the duration of the procession (a contractual arrangement not unlike the modern "masochistic contract," which we will take up later). The emphasis was on self-humiliation. The purpose was to gain forgiveness, but the ritualized processional floggings had the additional effect of intoxicating and charging the practitioners with a redemptive mission.

The Flagellants "saw their penance as a collective *imitatio Christi* possessing a unique, eschatological value."[18] The general populace also saw them as performing a collective penitential act which would hasten the world to the millenial reign of Christ while averting those catastrophes which threatened human annihilation. Thus masochism became a mode not only of redemption but also of survival. Crude, unsophisticated and too literal, perhaps, for modern taste, it nonetheless served as an effective and exalted way of dealing with an unreliable and terrifying world. And it seemed to work a transformation in many of those who participated.

It is too smug to speak of this Flagellant phenomenon as a "mass psychotic movement," or of its members as "malcontents" and "psychotics" and "maniacs."[19] Nothing is genuinely explained when a religious vocabulary ("virtue," "God," "sinfulness," "penance," "atonement") is merely replaced by a vocabulary of psychologisms ("superego ideals," "Father-figure," "unconscious guilt feelings," "need for punishment"). The phenomenon persists, in its service to necessity and soul. Pope Clement VI outlawed the Flagellants in 1349 for assorted heresies. But in the very next year, many of them were doing penance by being scourged by priests at the High Altar of St. Peter's in Rome, instead of by lay masters in the villages and cities. Flagellation continues in use today in some religious orders; as a form of penance, its purpose remains unaltered, though its place is unaltared in modern secular life.

Two former nuns of my acquaintance had been in religious orders which practiced the "Friday discipline," a private self-flagellation. Every Friday night they scourged their backs to discipline their souls. Yet both were troubled—in the telling perhaps more than in the doing—by the feelings they called "masochistic." Along with, and inseparable from, a desired union with the passion of Christ, and penance for that which separated them from him, were also vaguely pleasant sensations. These sensations, coupled with a subliminal and shameful anticipation of Friday nights, made these women consider their self-inflicted penance pleasurably masochistic, and therefore another sin to be punished. What was done in public processions six hundred years ago is now done in private cells, but the anticipation, the desire for it, the sexual undertone have somehow corrupted the religious experience for these two souls.

They suffer from psychology's dictum that religion is reducible to, and explainable by, the sexual instinct and its vicissitudes. They suffer too from the encultured idea that sexual feeling and religious feeling ought to be mutually exclusive. Yet the more the whipping, the more the uneasy pleasure in it, requiring still more penance. A shift of perspective, from either/or to both/and, would help us move out of the vicious cycle. Sex and body have been, perhaps, two of the basics that Christianity has not gotten down to.

The intrinsic part that sex and body play in the phenomenon of masochism will be covered in "Humiliation, or Getting Down to Basics" (Chapter 2). For now, suffice it to say that body has occupied a rather uncomfortable place within Christianity. Masochism, at a deeper level, may be one of psyche's efforts to make sex a sacrament—to keep body in spirituality. More spirit does not mean less body.

We can see that masochism, placed in a psychological context, embodies a religious attitude toward sexuality. It also embodies a religious attitude toward pain and suffering. As we all suffer, so we all have some attitude toward it. Sometimes we must take pause to discover our attitudes. In moments of sudden self-observance, we "overhear" our own words and tone as we talk, we take notice of a gesture, a posture, a gait, a tear. Sometimes it is the not-so-still voice within that says we hate our pain, we're mad or panicked to feel it, to have to deal with it again and again. Sometimes we note that we turn *toward* our pain, not away from it.

Masochism is an attitude which moves toward a dedication to suffering. The suffering I speak of here, with its religious resonance, is not so much the euphoria of suffering just to feel pain, nor the euphoria of knowing the pain will end soon and gratification is just around the corner. It is, rather, an attitude of dedication toward suffering which recognizes value and meaning in that suffering. Masochism can help lead a person to suffering for the sake of the soul's deeper knowledge of itself—a suffering toward, and of, *gnosis*. Self-knowledge hurts; anyone who has left the Garden of Eden knows this. Masochism, as one of the soul's fantasies of suffering, is an attitude which can lead to compassion, humility, and perhaps even healing, by referring the meaning of suffering ('pathology') back to its transpersonal source: those archetypes, or gods, who structure, afflict, and move the soul.

Thus, masochism may be seen as one manifestation of what Jung called "the religious instinct."[20] Psyche manifests its religious urge in myriad images and ideas, which come wrapped in mystery and numinosity, often compelling, sometimes dread-full and awe-full, ugly and fascinating. Masochistic experiences, too, are often touched with shades of these qualities. The seductive, alluring fascination of the *numen* is as much a part of masochistic experience as it is of religious experience.

Much of Catholic Christianity's liturgy, sacramental ritual, and theology is built on an awareness of, if not appreciation for, psychological (or religious) 'masochism.' In the central image of crucifixion we are confronted with the paradox of the pathology in redemption, and the redemption through *pathos*.[21] The *imitatio Christi* is a call not to punishment but to suffering. It exhibits itself in particular symbolic modes or stances: kneeling; hands together in prayer; bowing under the weight of one's cross; an outstretched, nailed-down exposure to death and redemption. It shows us an ongoing operation of mortification through examination of conscience, through contrition, confession, and penance.

The root meaning of the word "suffer" is "to bear" or "to carry," as a burden. Not all suffering refers to the personal ego. Often the deepest suffering comes not from bearing punishment, but from bearing *gnosis*, a constant burdensome knowledge of one's own truths and one's capacity for all manner of evil and destruction. Indeed, there is no paucity of opportunity to suffer in human life. No one need go looking for pain. Added to, and part of, *gnosis* is the profound suffering of helplessness, limitation, and powerlessness, in the recognition that even the best *imitatio Christi* remains an imitation. The Garden of Eden is God's doing, but Gethsemane is built with hard and private labor.

In the same way we were able to perceive the suffering, ecstatic Flagellant behind the modern masochist, we can also discern the outlines of some fundamental Christian concepts (suffering, repentance, atonement, sacrifice) behind masochistic phenomena. Of course masochism becomes pathological when it is a surface phenomenon, a superficiality, with no backdrop, no reference to a deeper ground. We might imagine that we are beyond the worship of ancient Greek gods, and that

> we have left all these phantasmal gods far behind. But what we have left behind are only verbal spectres, not the psychic facts that were responsible for the birth of the gods. We are still as much possessed by autonomous psychic contents as if they were Olympians. Today they are called phobias, obsessions, and so forth; in a word, neurotic symptoms. The gods have become diseases; Zeus no longer rules Olympus but rather the solar plexus, and produces curious specimens for the doctor's consulting room. . . . It is not a matter of indifference whether one calls something a "mania" or a "god." To serve a mania is detestable and undignified, but to serve a god is full of meaning and promise because it is an act of submission to a higher, invisible, and spiritual being. . . . When the god is not acknowledged, ego-mania develops, and out of this mania comes sickness.[22]

When masochism is literal only, it is pathological. Without its sense of worship and submission, without acknowledgment of the god moving in it, masochism loses its connection to, and meaning for, the soul. Unconscious of deeper motives and soul needs, we see only sin in unreflective sadomasochistic sex. Religious suffering looks like perversion; repentance like excessive, fruitless guilt (another form of egocentricity); atonement like one-sided moralism (a way of denying genuine suffering and paradox); crucifixion like martyrdom (the ego in a fantasy of persecuted heroism); and sacrifice like self-mutilation, an infliction of literal and physical pain in a bloody effort to redeem oneself (an idolatrous way of attributing divine power to the ego).

Suffering, repentance, atonement, and sacrifice, whether or not they are cast in a specifically Christian framework, are fundamental psychological experiences. They may be humiliating to the ego, but they are of profound import and meaning—and sometimes intense pleasure—to the soul. These experiences may bring humility and healing. Masochism requires that we stay with the down-and-under side of Christianity. The image of crucifixion pierces us with its paradox of redeeming torment. But as traditionally interpreted, it carries us only so far and then ceases to serve as a precise image of masochism. Orthodoxy requires that, eventually, the psychology of Good Friday be supplanted by the theology of Easter. Masochism is more concerned with death than with resurrection; it finds deliverance and redemption *in* mortification and mortality, not only afterwards.

A Deflection:
Masochism and Modern American Psychotherapy

The recognition of value and meaning in the desire to suffer humiliation runs counter to the generally prevailing attitude in psychology. Regardless of theoretical school or therapeutic technique, the main thrust of modern theory and practice has been toward ego psychology. The values of psychotherapy have been aimed, for the most part, at building strong, coping, rational, problem-solving egos. Notice that these are attitudes which the ego has defined for itself. At present, we know a great deal more about this part of personality called ''ego,'' its defenses, ambitions, and goals, than we know about the defenses, intentions, and processes of the rest of the soul. Ego-values are certainly worthy ones, yet it costs something to gain strength, to cope, to be rational, and to solve problems. The expense has been borne by other values, other psychic figures.

''For us,'' laments Carl Schneider, ''the world is a problem to be solved, not a mystery to be respected.''[23] But from a deeper perspective, as a psychiatrist colleague phrased it, ''some problems have only portrayals, not solutions.''[24] For insoluble problems, solutions formulated by, and comprehensible to, the ego are betrayals of the deeper soul and its questions of meaning. In depth psychology, when we move to the mythic realm, the fantasy of 'problems' and 'solutions' is relatively unimportant. Conflicts, needs, passions exist—but as portraits, eternal scenarios. In myth, the soul portrays itself, and each portrait has all it needs.

Modern therapy begins with the ego—whether in interpreting dreams or understanding schizophrenia—and ends with it as well. From weak ego to strong ego makes a small circle. This vicious cycle may account for the dissatisfaction many people feel after weeks, months, or even years of psychotherapy. Building a strong ego is only one side of the mountain, the upward climb; but some small quiet voice down below is always asking, a la Betty Friedan years ago, "Is this all there is?"

Modern psychology has been in large measure dominated by the archetype of the hero, its chief attitude and goal being "heroic consciousness." This is one archetypal pattern appearing in "feelings of independence, strength, and achievement, in ideas of decisive action, coping, planning, virtue, conquest (over animality), and in psychopathologies of battle, overpowering masculinity, and single-mindedness."[25] Much of the modern therapeutic vocabulary is heroic battle-language: we speak of "confrontation," "defense mechanism," "anxiety attacks," "marshaling" or "mobilization of resources" ("getting it all together"), "retreat" and "regression," "advance" (growth and notions of progress), being "shot down." We are imperialistic toward our dreams. "I had a dream," we say, not, "A dream had me." And having viewed the dream as servant to the ego, we then discover 'messages' in dreams addressed special delivery to the ego, readily deciphered by us with a bit of rationalism and wit. We do almost anything but 'surrender,' which we equate with giving in or losing the battle.

Societally, the heroic ego in America rides on in glory, usually oblivious to the hard reality that every silver lining has a cloud. Weakness or failure of nerve (and depression) go against American traditions of rugged individualism, Horatio Algerism, Manifest Destiny, Big Stickism, and the Pride of the Corps. In the last decades, the American heroic ego has suffered the defeats of Vietnam, Watergate, the energy crisis, and the Iranian hostage situation. The hero is getting tired, and it is getting harder to tell the difference between real golden glory and mere gold plating. Manifest Destiny has diminished to hanging on to what we've got; the Big Stick is a mere twig against OPEC dominance.

But clearly, to survive in a non-Hollywood world, the American ego must deal with wider realities. Like a one-sidedly neurotic individual, America could benefit from a more grounded, more flexible attitude. Rather than the solitary stance of heroic consciousness, we need a round table of power and experience. Not the rightness of the Moral Majority, but a little humility would help.

Culturally, there are similar themes. In the 1960s and 1970s, these shifted from "America First," "Peace Above All" and "Justice for All" to "Me First." This is called the "Me Generation," and "Me" is synonymous with "ego." The ego realm is the realm of personal concern, where one takes care of oneself first. Its psychology revolves around claiming one's space, taking responsibility, "owning" all that is within, making a choice, asserting oneself. We encourage and encounter, give and receive "ego-strokes," try to "feel good about ourselves," and struggle heroically to "take control of our lives"—as if control must be wrested with Herculean strength away from Fate or God or The Government. It is the ego which assumes these heroic efforts will eliminate personal guilt and personal failure. It is the ego which believes more control will give us the Promethean daring to rise to peak—not descend to depth—experiences.

Never has therapy been so common, and so assertion-minded. Yet there is an emptiness that all this variety and all these assertions have not been able to fill. The "Me Generation" seems to know it has missed something. Its collective and active approach has resulted in groups for sensitization, awareness, realization—all aiming toward being more In Touch and All There. But in a culture like ours, where so much happens in an instant—coffee, printing, replays, self-knowledge in crash weekends—we forget that expansion may happen by decay and slow rot as well as by active effort. We forget that we need passivity training as much as assertiveness training. The psyche is also *im*personal (not-I) and *trans*personal (more-than-I). Ego cannot speak to the deeper sense of dissatisfaction unless it is willing to descend to the base, the basics and baseness, and also to the collectivity of life apart from its exclusive concerns.

Masochism moves 'down' and 'out,' counter to the values and goals of ego psychology. Its directions can radically alter the ego-attitude—by moving away from, or out of, egocentricity.

Masochism is a fantasy of being struck, not stroked, of pleasure in feeling bad, of abdicating control. Masochism acknowledges other gods, gods with radically different perspectives on suffering, perhaps gods like Christ or Dionysus who personify suffering. Masochism carries a radical anti-ego message: there are gods in our sickness who relieve us of the tedious and boring demand for good feeling; there are gods who, in the worst moments of torment and humiliation, remind us that we are, emphatically and constitutionally, *not okay*.

Masochism is an operation of negatives, a focus on that which is negative (not to be construed as bad, evil, or undesirable). It centers on lack, inadequacy, and weakness. We feel scornful of this, as of the ninety-pound weakling, forgetting that his equally one-sided opposite, the muscle-bound bully, is also decidedly unattractive.

I have found in practice and research that often the masochist is not an inferior. In fact, the reverse seems to be the case. Masochists are more likely to be successful by social standards: professionally, sexually, emotionally, culturally, in marriage or out. They are frequently individuals of admirable inner strength of character, possessed of strong "coping egos" and with an ethical sense of individual responsibility. Perhaps the very presence of these qualities makes their masochism understandable and necessary. One notices in these personalities a strong discomfort with their own image of success. Masochism, by combining humiliation and pleasure in one experience, makes for ambivalence, and thus helps prevent a one-sided attitude—too much belief in one's competence, too much faith in one's abilities. Instead of needing to be cured, masochism may lead to a cure for a one-sided ego which might otherwise drown in its own accomplishments.

This notion of 'curing' deserves attention. It is, after all, the main focus of psychotherapy. When, characteristically, we turn our attention down and back, we find the words "curiosity" and "cure" come from the same root. The Latin *cura* means "care," "trouble," "anxiety," "concern," "sorrow," "attention (to)" and "concern (for)." Insofar as masochism is experienced as something deviant, it irresistibly arouses our curiosity. This very curiosity may prepare us for moving deeper into the dark, unfathomable recesses of soul.

It is a hard thing in therapy to foster care and concern for that masochistic part of one's personality, for that 'perverse' desire to be wounded and humiliated and to enjoy it in some measure. Yet curiosity is essential and may begin a therapeutic process which is less interested in killing or eliminating the 'perversion' than it is in understanding and loving it.

> The relationship between cure and curiosity . . . suggests that these are not to be kept apart. Perhaps the cure comes when one is motivated by curiosity to go into the pathology rather than away from it.[26]

There is a value in keeping the idea of deviance when we consider masochism: "deviations . . . become cues to the essence of individuality."[27] As Guggenbühl-Craig points out, masochism is better understood with the concept of individuation:

> Is not the suffering of our life, and of life in general, one of the most difficult things there is to accept? The world is full of suffering, and all of us suffer so greatly in body and spirit, that even the saints have difficulty understanding this. It is one of the most difficult tasks of the individuation process to accept sorrow and joy, pain and pleasure, God's anger and God's grace. The opposites—suffering and joy, pain and pleasure—are symbolically united in masochism. Thus life can be actually accepted, and even pain can be joyfully experienced. The masochist, in a remarkable and fantastic way, confronts and comes to terms with the greatest opposites of our existence.[28]

Patients have been accused of expecting too much from psychotherapy. But perhaps psychotherapy, in the smallness of its vision, has expected too little of patients. We have brought masochism to psychotherapy to be cured. We need instead to recognize the soul-need in its downward movement, and the passion and need in its extremity. Masochism is a natural product of soul, ready and needing to bring forward its own vision and its own cure.

CHAPTER 2

Humiliation, or Getting Down to Basics

> The way out of the labyrinth is to
> keep your hand on the cold,
> damp, shuddering wall of your
> humiliation.
>
> NOR HALL, "Labyrinths"

> But there ain't no answers up in the sky,
> We got to give the earth a try.
> You got to get down a little closer to the
> ground.
>
> TONI BROWN, "Closer to the Ground"

Clinical evidence and pornography indicate two primary elements which comprise masochistic experience: humiliation and pleasure. Though an incomplete definition of masochism, this does give some specificity: wherever we feel both humiliation and pleasure at roughly the same time, there we are experiencing masochism.

Some people seem to charge, or clatter, through humiliating experiences. They ignore, cover, deny, or take up arms against humiliating aspects of living. It is humiliating to be hurt by a lover or parent, defeated by an enemy or friend. It brings waves of shame to realize that one has been used—by a lover, a friend, a corporation—and that our own, as well as another's, greediness or blindness has entrapped us. There are the degradations of failed hopes, shameful memories, the inability to cope, the weakness in crisis. And there is the humiliation of physical and emotional pain, illness and—looming large at the end—the final defeat, death.

It is *hubris*, false pride, to pretend that the low side of life isn't there, or isn't really low. Full humanity, of course, requires experience of this down side of life along with the up side. We hope to be saved from the down side by turning to professions, groups, mates, money. As a kind of prototype of all of us, psychotherapy patients approach therapy with the hope that they will be 'cured' of their weaknesses, mistakes and shame. They feel humiliated, and often the therapist does too—inadequate and too small to meet this tormented soul on its own ground. To start therapy at all, to ask for help, is often humiliating, a recognition that one is in need—like the imprinting of a stigma which only much later, if the gods are kind, becomes a stigmata, a mark of divine favor.

The word "humiliation," rich in meaning, comes from the Latin word *humus*, which means "earth" or "ground." Humus is the dark organic material in soils, produced by the decomposition of vegetable or animal matter. It is essential to the earth's fertility. Humiliation, then, is a process of decay and decomposition, of matter's feeling rotten. That which is dark and soiled in us, which decomposes and causes us to lose our composure, becomes fertilizing material, life-giving, vital.

Wallowing in dirt can also be gardening. Masochism may be imagined as cultivation of what Jung called the shadow[1]—of suffering the shadow, opening oneself to it, submitting to its reality. The shadow is best understood and experienced through our dream figures and relationships, more accurately portrayed in the personified images than described in conceptual language: it is one principal person of psyche rather than a principle of personality. Any one person has many kinds of shadows. In dreams, one form of shadow might appear as a figure that we abhor and despise—someone nasty, cruel, uncaring, or weak, or stupid. In outer relationships, one feels similarly to a person who "carries one's shadow." One loudly disowns someone's bossiness or boisterousness or pettiness, protesting too much. There, in those very qualities which seem most foreign and detestable, lurk our shadows. When they reach us through our own flashes of insight, or through the perceptions of others, we are subjected to humiliation.

The shadow appears to have intentionality, as do other psychic figures, usually thwarting the ego's intentions, frustrating and humiliating them. Very often, it feels perverse, and it takes a kind of perversion to explore it. Yet let us remember the intimate connection between curiosity and caring and curing. "Perversion," from the Latin words *per* ("through") and *versare* ("to keep turning," "to twist," "to upset" or "to disturb"), means "to turn through"; thus this style of embracing and suffering the shadow is a turning through, an internal sifting, twisting, and contorting through shadowy matters and material. One turns oneself inside out. In embracing the shadow, one does not get off lightly.

Jung said the shadow connects an individual to the collective unconscious, and beyond that to animal life at its most primitive level. The shadow is the tunnel, channel, or connector through which one reaches the deepest, most elemental layers of psyche. Going through the tunnel, or bringing the ego down, one feels reduced, even degraded, to an animal.

Usually, we try to bring the shadow under the ego's domination, which is, in one way, a sadistic attitude of heroic ego-consciousness. Embracing the shadow, on the other hand, does not aim to dominate it or make it more acceptable. Let us say, for example, that one man's shadow quality is arrogance. It is repugnant to him when he sees it in others and unacceptable and embarrassing when he sees it in himself. This arrogance cannot be diminished or made more acceptable to this man's ego by will-power; massive doses of modesty cannot offset it. But it can be modified by understanding it. In order to come to a deeper sense of his own substance, the man must get to know this shadow and learn its intentions.

"Embracing the shadow" does not necessarily mean acting it out. It is more like a dance-embrace, with timing and rhythm, give-

and-take. Experiencing the shadow means accepting its life within us—letting it, and thus ourselves, live. "Experience" comes from the Latin *(ex periculum)* meaning "to move through peril" or "out of danger." Embracing the shadow means experiencing its autonomy. It involves force and passivity, horror and beauty, power and impotence, straightness and perversion, infantilism, wisdom, and banality.

The experience of the shadow is humiliating, and occasionally frightening, but it is a reduction to life—essential life. The shadow is a psychopomp or guide to the nether regions. In Jungian terms, the shadow leads back to those archetypes that are one's basic nature, that are the centers of one's complexes, that form the foundations and contexts of one's personality. The shadow experience is a lowering to a more solid ground than ego-consciousness alone. It is a reduction, a leading back (not a "reductive interpretation") to origins.

Perhaps there is no place we feel our basic qualities, our essential natures, more than in our physical bodies. This place of the body is where we come face to face with the lengths and depths we go to in order to obtain love, attention, recognition, food, money, sex, a raise, a drink, a cigarette. Shadow enacts itself in the body as physical postures and symptoms. Masochism relies heavily on the body to give it voice. It enacts itself in the body through spoken words of submission, and through gestures and postures of weakness and shame—bowed heads, covered eyes, bent knees. In my practice, I have seen several sets of symptoms which turned out to be related to, or expressions of, masochism in this psychological sense. These symptoms, bodily images of psychological masochistic movement, range from stiff necks (which won't bow) to troublesome knees (which won't bend or carry weighty soul-matter) to back pain (forcing one to lie prostrate) to stomach cramps and nausea (forcing one to double over, unable to stomach the matter).

These kinds of symptoms carry the pain of the masochistic complex, its emotion, vulnerability, uncontrollability, weakness. They persist, with—and because of—the obstinacy of pride, until we are brought low in our helplessness to attend to them, and to understand their importance and meaning. Besieged by a migraine headache, one is laid low. Every heartbeat, every emotion, every smell and sound implodes. The world becomes an unbearably violent and excessively vibrant place, where only total retreat and immobility are possible. Sleep, darkness, silence. . . . Submission to the pain must be complete.

Body symptoms are psychologically expressive as well as literally somatic. Psychologically understood, body language is soul language; treatment of symptoms for the sake of symptom-relief too often results in neglect of the deeper experience of the soul speaking in them. 'Curing' body symptoms may deprive the soul of its voice. The healing is in the wound itself, as the old saying has it, and it may be that we need to learn how to *suffer* painful complexes and complexities more than to *eliminate* them. Like Jacob, who wrestled with the angel, we are changed by being ''put out of joint,'' and we carry the experience and lessons of the wound, limping, for the rest of our lives.

Feelings of humiliation, of course, find their images in enormous variety in dreams and fantasies. Another group of body images comes from the language and art of sexual masochism. These include the body in bondage (the impressive variety of leather and chains and instruments of bondage), the body being whipped or beaten, the body prostrate, the body dominated by rape, and a whole spectrum of submissive postures, from head-bowing to foot-kissing.

When we see submissive postures in sexual activities, we call them masochistic; when we see them in church, we call them religious. From a psychological perspective, these embodiments are two modes of the same phenomenon: the soul expressing itself either in sexual metaphors or religious metaphors, or both at the same time. In religion, we find the bondage motif in Jesus bound before Pilate, St. Peter in chains, the heretic bound to the stake. For flagellation we again have Jesus being scourged, the worshippers of Dionysus whipped ritually with the holy thyrsus, the penitential self-floggings in monasteries and convents. For domination by rape, we have the highly erotic testimonies of saints like Teresa of Avila and poets like John Donne, who have been "ravished" by the Holy Spirit. And for the spectrum of submissive postures, we have the commonest enactments of worship: bowed heads, bent knees, folded hands, covered heads, and Islamic prostration. Formerly, Roman Catholic cardinals kissed the Pope's foot in homage; we have already seen this enactment, down to its very details, in one of Masoch's most erotic images. Even Christian tradition does not endorse an only-upward movement of the soul to God, earth to heaven. "Thus humiliation is the way to humility," says St. Bernard of Clairvaux, and "without humility, nothing is pleasing to God," says St. Francis of Assisi.

For several centuries, our souls have been disembodied. In the swing from the Victorian era back to body in this century, we have lost the soul. The body's materiality—indeed, the materiality of everything—has become our culture's preoccupation. And yet, the very matter *of* the body has become the matter *with* it: idealized in its material form, like an idol, it is accorded every pleasure, receives sacrifices (diets, exercises), and exacts tribute (millions of dollars of the Gross National Product). Body products have become one of the biggest markets around. The search—and the stretch—for new and different body-experiences goes on and on: vibrators for every part of the body, redwood hot tubs, multiple shower-heads, do-it-to-yourself Jacuzzis and whirlpools, styles of massage ranging from gentle to violent, even "total environment" systems which simulate rain and sun, give thirty-second tans, etc. Lately there has been a particularly strong surge in healthful body consciousness: you can buy a myriad of programs and books on healthful diets, healthful exercise, healthful mental attitudes.

Yet we know that soul and body occur simultaneously in our lives. Perhaps the fact that we have tended to separate them, and to "put down" the body as inferior, accounts in part for the body's heavy importance to the masochistic experience. In masochism, *embodiment keeps image and behavior together*, so that soul experience is all of a piece. It brings image-essence and material-essence together in flesh-and-blood experience, a down-to-earth essence. Like masochism, our embodiment is an existence full of both paradox and power.

Masochistic reduction of the ego, to basics, to shadow, to body, is a baseline experience. It seems to be a necessary process—less, perhaps, for sexual pleasure than for the humus of psychic earth, for the very health and vitality of the soul. As much as most people would abhor the idea, masochistic experience does radical therapy, performs radical change on the ego. A masochistic posture strips down and exposes the ego—its defenses, ambitions, failures, and successes. It is a psychological *posture* in which we are humiliated, brought down, made defenseless, made aware that we must die. Through masochism we can sometimes contact the deeper meaning in the suffering, the depth of its pain and pleasure. If our submission is genuine, we can feel it is for the sake of something greater, more important, more valuable than the ego and its perceptions. The ego becomes servant to that greater thing. This 'something' may be called by many different names, depending on one's personal psychological orientation and temperament. One may submit to the whole personality, the Self, psyche, soul, or God. The necessity and desirability of submission—the chief characteristic of masochism—is a submission to Necessity herself, the Goddess Ananke. No wonder, then, that masochism is so hard to 'cure.'

As a matter of fact, to make things both better and worse, *any* archetype, not only the shadow, may demand submission. Every complex, every troublesome psychological situation, has a god in it demanding attention, forcing its own intention upon us. The gods are our fate, and whither shall we flee from their presence? We are stamped with their images, marked by them. The heavy hand of Saturn is on us no matter how liberated we may be from the Father, from Time, from historical roots. Mars will have his due, no matter how much we rise above martial strife, family feuds, and temper tantrums. Hermes will be served, no matter how respectable, straight, and up-front we wish to be. We learn to submit voluntarily to the divinities of soul, in which case we find meaning and dignity. Submission to the greater-than-ego aspect happens, whether our submission is voluntary or not. If we are forced, our intentions become compulsions and our behavior, repetitiously neurotic. In most therapeutic work, the primary task is to pass through compulsive to voluntary submission.

Masochistic experience can mark a moment of divine revelation—when Eros is present. One of Eros's names means ''He who reveals.'' Eros's revelation makes possible a new or different relationship between ego and unconscious psyche. It makes possible a different style of consciousness. In our times, ego is hero, with assertion and logic and will-power his domain. But a wider consciousness—including domination *and* subjection—becomes almost violently necessary for the sake of the whole soul. Soul-need knocks, impinges, assaults from many varied places, but most often from the contexts we have mentioned, religion and psychology. Wider consciousness makes its demands in born-again Christianity, born-again paganism, religious cults of all kinds, perhaps even in rock 'n' roll concerts, mass sports events and drug use. This same soul seeks its breadth in all manner of therapies. People meet in dyads, triads, couples' groups and large audiences; they hear speakers, see films, take tests, make testimonials, and discuss everything. They encounter, intervene, convene, touch, reveal, hold, confront, massage, surrender, talk, beat, fall, scream, and talk some more. However bizarre they appear in a list, all of these experiences may lead to a new relationship between ego and the whole soul, a wider consciousness.

If it is to bring depth as well as breadth, this revelation entails humiliation—a price nearly always too high for proud ego to pay. It is much higher than a therapist's fee. It is so high, in fact, that the willingness, the desire to pay it, is itself considered symptomatic of low self-esteem or even pathology.

Seeing is knowing. The eyes are the organs of humiliation and shame: one is seen, exposed, and one sees oneself, not with a casual glance but with acute penetration. This is not the gaze of narcissistic infatuation, but the perception of the lower self, the much-less-than-noble, even sordid, sloughs of psyche. These include the fantasies of what we call sick perversion, grotesque desires, which lie beneath the dark protective wings of the goddess *Aidos* (Shame); to have them exposed is to die of shame. It is in these night secrets that we are most vulnerable; our halting, shamefaced confessions and admissions made to a close friend, a priest, an analyst, or a bartender are the most revealing things we can say about ourselves. And yet they are at the same time springs of depth from which we can draw endless insight and understanding.

This revelation of and to oneself, this close looking, differs markedly from narcissism. The image of Narcissus gazing into the quiet pool with love and longing does not describe the experience of shame in seeing oneself and being seen. Instead of causing us to languish pool-side, the ambivalence of shame throws us into all manner of conflict and confusion.

The burning glare of shame, so different in quality from the cool wetness of narcissism, belies the traditional view of masochism as narcissistic and immature. Psychoanalysis has followed Freud's lead in seeing masochism through a negative version of the child archetype, finding in it childish irresponsibility, stunted growth, infantile sexuality, and failure to reconcile the ego to parental demands in the form of superego conflicts.

But even if we follow Freud in assuming that the origins of masochism lie in childhood, in a state of incomplete development, we may imagine masochism as leading toward completion in adulthood. The ability to hold paradox and ambivalence, and to experience impossible unions, belongs to maturity. These attributes, intrinsic parts of the experience of masochism, transcend childhood's irreconcilable conflicts. Masochism in the mature adult can be an ongoing process of drying out, a shifting from free-flowing ego-guilt to a hot, dry sense of shame in the soul. The residue of each masochistic experience is ash, stored in little piles in the hidden, deep recesses of the soul, in its history and memory, and each of these dried, preserved experiences can be sifted again and again. If the narcissist spends his eternal youth near the water, drowning in love, the masochist reaches maturity by fire, burned and scarred, his damp narcissistic identifications evaporated in the heat of shame and humiliation, his delusions of power, purity, and beauty reduced to ash.

In one sense at least, it is the quality of *recognition* which sets up narcissism and masochism as contrasts. The narcissist does not recognize the substance of his own reflected self in the water, and so does not recognize the quality of reflection in his own soul. Watery vision, misty thinking, sentimental infatuation—these aspects of narcissism give only a shimmering picture and a surface reflection. However, the reflection in a mirror—a favorite prop of masochists—is exact, clear, and backed with mercury, the alchemical element of psychic reflection. The mirror gives a reflection of depth without distortion. The masochist sees not a stranger, but his own soul, and the accuracy of the reflection forces it upon him. There is a real pleasure in this, and a real humiliation: one's own darkness and need may be ignoble, but at least they are as essential as earth, and one's own. As the song says,

> You got to get down a little closer to the ground.
> People everywhere are goin' out of their minds
> Looking for answers in symbols and signs,
> But there ain't no answers up in the sky
> We got to give the earth a try.
> . . . .
> If you can't feel pain then you can't feel love,
> You gotta let go of what you're thinking of,
> Because you're too far away from where you were
>   at birth
> You better get down to earth.[2]

CHAPTER 3

Pleasure, or The Play's The Thing

*The greatest pleasures are born of
conquered repugnancies.*
MARQUIS DE SADE

*Now you're a real tough cookie with a
  long history
Of breaking little hearts like the one in
  me.
That's okay—let's see how you do it,
Put up your dukes, let's get down to it.*

*Hit me with your best shot—
Fire away.*
PAT BENATAR, "Hit Me With Your Best Shot"

The perversity of masochism is the mainspring of its pleasure.
The sense of the perverse, the aberrant, the abnormal, the deviant is
exciting. After all, to be normal is to be like everyone, but to be
perverse is to be one of a kind. Abnormality makes for individuality
and uniqueness. The particular ways that individuals express their
masochism are as much distinguishing characteristics as their taste
in clothes, food, music.

People who come to therapy for masochism are asking for help in
dealing with its pleasure as much as its pain. They are already suffering from the social stigma attached to deviants and from
psychiatry's pronouncement that masochism is a sickness. But this
sense of sickness is not only social and medical; it is inherent in the
experience of masochism as part of its pleasure and pain. It is hard
for people to say, "I hurt"; it is much harder to admit, "I enjoy
feeling hurt." This simultaneous pain and pleasure creates an

unbearable contradiction, and to make it bearable, we 'normally' attempt to deny at least one side.

To feel sick is to feel close to something profoundly human: limited, inadequate, inferior, even shameful. To feel bittersweet, poignant pleasure in this sickness—even joy—keeps one close to this deep, interior sense of limitation, inadequacy, and shame. That we condemn masochism as perverse perhaps reveals less about masochists than it does about our collective attitude toward our basic, profound humanity: we have not accepted, and certainly not solved, the dilemma of being more and less than human. Pain and pleasure go inextricably together, defying logic, rationality, reasonableness—all those things we equate with sanity. There is no cure for this sickness and its pleasure, and perhaps there ought to be none. The perverse quality gives masochism its odd texture; it is the fabric of which masochism is made.

For Freud, the pleasure principle governed the desire for immediate gratification; "immediacy rules the polymorphous realm," notes Patricia Berry.[1] And the polymorphous conjures up the realm of the perverse child, so that masochism is just another in the family of infantilisms, like narcissism and measles and dirty diapers. But masochistic experience requires further differentiation, for its pleasure is of a specific kind. While masochism may indeed be polymorphous in its variety of fantasy-shapes, it comes in adult sizes. Each masochistic experience is specific and singular, as is each pleasure.

Most masochists do not engage in literal, physical pain; they are, in fact, repelled by the thought. The pleasure in masochism is strongly anticipatory. Masoch's masochist is highly stimulated by anticipating what his mistress will do next with him: "I am . . . experiencing those things that . . . have always filled me with such sweet fear. What senseless apprehension! . . . How exquisite is this agonizing doubt!"[2]

The source of pleasure is not pain, but humiliation, and its anticipation is the spice. The most thrilling element, write Gerald and Caroline Greene, is ". . . often the waiting, the apprehension. 'This suspense is dreadful,' as a lady in an Oscar Wilde play puts it, 'I do hope that it lasts.' There is, in short, pleasure, awaiting somewhere beyond this agonizing, yet so delectable, anticipation."[3] In everyday terms, we may find ourselves in the middle of a fantasy of hurt or humiliation, repeat a certain scene, worsen it, amplify it, heighten it. So there is pleasure not only "awaiting beyond," but pleasure *in* the agonizing anticipation. Theodor Reik calls this the "suspense factor" in masochism. He concludes that "masochistic pleasure is more dependent on this expectation of discomfort than on discomfort itself."[4]

Literature on masochism notes that masochists usually repeat their fantasies. This repetition is not just a symptom of masochism's compulsive and perverse nature. It is, more importantly, a process of *refinement*. Masochists change the "hows" and "whys" and "whens" and "to-whoms" of submission constantly to yield varied and maximum pleasure. They refine their fantasies again and again to bring new satisfactions. This is so obvious that it bears repeating. Repetition is a mode of refining, a psychological operation to refine, impress, solidify, make an experience stick. Gratifications, whether immediate or postponed, do not last forever; pleasures, too, ". . . wear themselves out. . . . Pleasures grow weary of themselves and then seek new refinements in order to become again pleasurable. . . . Pleasure has in itself its own differentiation, and, in fact, pleasure demands it."[5]

The pleasure in a psychological masochistic experience is not dependent upon, nor can it be reduced to, an exclusively sensual pleasure—though the two may be metaphorically similar. Here again in masochism we meet with the body in soul experience and soul in body experience. We might call masochistic pleasure an imaginal sensuality, following Masoch: "I am a super-sensualist; with me everything takes root in the imagination and finds its nourishment there."[6] Similarly, the psychological experience of masochism is not identical with the sexual pleasure of physical arousal and orgasm. But it is *like* a sexual pleasure in that it delights in foreplay, builds to a release and a letting go. They are similar—not quite identical—experiences, especially if they are a letting go and falling. Masochistic pleasure is *like* looking at Michelangelo's Pieta—it is so beautiful and poignant that it hurts. It is *like* being emotionally charged, and especially sensitive, painfully aware of and pleasured by one's own vitality and substance.

Masochism brings a very real pleasure too when its humiliation results in the loss of old ego-constructs. One lets go of old, worn-out self-images and attitudes. In masochism, they go to hell. Sometimes the satisfaction entails a release of tension from the need to defend the ego. In the quiet of night, in loneliness, in stray moments at stoplights and on elevators, we may finally give in to and admit to our mistakes and inadequacies. These momentary 'breakdowns' allow release of that which has been held back (repressed), and the effect is to make us, not morally better, but more flexible and receptive to what the soul needs.

Because a 'good confession' brings the same sort of relief, confession is good for the soul. The Roman Catholic Church has divided the sacrament of Penance into three parts: contrition, confession, and satisfaction. "Satisfaction" means repayment or rectification, as satisfaction to God for sins against him. But there is a psychological satisfaction of the soul that comes from confessing, from letting down one's guard. It is not so much that the presence of another person makes confession more humiliating; it is that the other's presence makes humiliation more real, for that presence makes for immediacy, awareness, acute sensitivity. Between the observable stammerings and fidgetings, there is little room for self-deception.

The eyes have it; there is less escape into illusion. In the humanity of the other we meet our own finite, limited, inadequate, human selves. Sometimes that meeting, that common bond, gives added pleasure, and sometimes even joy.

Letting go of one's habitual defenses does two things at once: it leaves one feeling vulnerable, weak, humiliated, and perhaps disoriented; it also leaves one feeling relieved and pleasantly satisfied at having the trappings removed—the superficialities that entrap us—so that the truth, the substance, the essential reality of one's personality can come through.

It is as if the soul needs to know the truth about itself, needs to know its reality. Masochism can be understood as a way of meeting this need, in that it fosters receptivity. This receptivity to soul is what makes its reality possible. In one of her writings, Simone Weil said it is impossible for us to forgive anyone who does us harm if we are degraded by it; so we must think that the harm has not degraded us, but has revealed some true level. This is also true when we humiliate and harm ourselves. If we are to forgive ourselves, we must somehow understand the experience as a realization or revelation. One of the pleasures of a masochistic experience can be that it leads to the satisfaction of reaching a true level, of finding deep and low-down truths about oneself.

*

We must also consider the aesthetics of masochism, a pleasure that is both beautiful and painful at the same time. When we speak of someone as "a beautiful person," we refer not to an appearance but to a quality of soul. Most often it is the soul in the dignity of its humility which we find beautiful. We need not fear being caught up in moral overtones here, for humility has always been recognized as the hallmark of the soul. "Soul-making," to use James Hillman's phrase,[7] makes for humility, as it requires a continual relativizing of the ego.

During the Romantic era, which saw the birth of Masoch and the death of the Marquis de Sade, "painful beauty" was a characteristic configuration, putting agony into romantic imagination and romance into agonizing fantasy. The Romantics looked upon Beauty and Death as sisters. They became "fused into a sort of two-faced herm, filled with corruption and melancholy and fatal in its beauty—a beauty of which, the more bitter the taste, the more abundant the enjoyment."[8]

Corruption, melancholy, fate, beauty and death: these are the colors and tones of masochism. They give it both its apparent excess of passion, and an imaginal structure or order for this excess. Art, fantasy, and ritual provide forms for the soul's emotional images. That which is important to an artist is equally important to a masochistic fantasy: composition or arrangement, mood or feeling-tone, syntax, timing. "There is no specifically masochistic phantasy, but rather a masochistic art of phantasy."[9] Masochism yields pleasure through casting itself as fantasy in artful form and ritual.

Since the time of Krafft-Ebing one hundred years ago, we have paid so much attention to masochism in literal sex that we have neglected masochism as artful fantasy, as a psychological and aesthetic activity. Precisely this sexual literalism, which we find in contemporary, pornographic 'S-M' magazines, results in loss of the aesthetic. What remains on the newsstands are high-priced, low-grade photographic exhibitions, lacking subtlety, Eros, and imagination. They also lack the sense of apprehension and shame that go with genuine masochistic exhibitionism. These are posed photographic exposures, not exposures of the soul. The sorry quality of pornography presents us with a stern fact: when we keep refusing masochism recognition as a psychological experience, it does not go away but goes anywhere it can.

Masoch's works have an aesthetic sense in them, and an aesthetic appreciation is present, however obscured or misidentified, in most masochistic art, drama, literature, fantasy. There is a ritualistic—and one might add artistic and religious—quality in fantasies of masochism: everything must be 'right' to achieve the effect. The great importance of ritual has led the psychoanalytical tradition to place masochism in the category of an obsessive-compulsive neurosis.[10] But the primacy of ritual also signifies a kind of religiosity, as in the following fantasy of a modern woman:

> I regally and serenely present myself in front of a huge audience for the ritual piercing of my nipples with hot needles, after which huge rings are inserted. More recently this has expanded, so that in taking a simple bath I am being prepared for an elaborate ritual of circumcision, ceremonial rape, and final sacrifice (by disemboweling) to some awesome god.[11]

The scene, the fantasy, is specific. It is a highly particularized, individually defined experience. The coming together of humiliation and pleasure happens only in a certain way, at a certain time. In the form of age-old religious sacrifices, this woman presents herself as a human sacrifice. Like Iphigenia, like Christ, like the Vestal Virgins, like an offering to Moloch, she partakes, in her fantasy, in the solemn and exciting drama of submission to collective and godlike will.

Specific artistry and ritual are evident in most, if not all, developed fantasies. The more imaginatively crafted the fantasy, the clearer and more apparent are its ritual features. For another example, we turn again to Leopold von Sacher-Masoch.

In his most philosophically complete novel, *Venus in Furs*, actual sexual intercourse ranks far behind the whippings and humiliations the protagonist demands and receives from his mistress—and even these, to be satisfying, depend on the composition of the scene in which they happen. Masoch's attention to detail is striking: the hero must enter the room at a certain time, certain clothes must be worn, the furniture and paintings must be arranged in a certain way. And there is a mirror. Masoch, like all good masochists, captures the moment—a glance in the mirror arrests the moment, etching the image in memory for later reflection. The total effect is a high sense of anticipation, sensuality, and aesthetics. Everything is beautifully in order, the stage is set, the play may begin.

The artistic fantasy of masochism is not only or always visual. Sometimes it centers around certain words, which must be spoken with certain emphases and in a certain tone of voice. Theodor Reik calls those for whom speech is the occasion of titillation "verbal masochists" and gives this comment and example:

> Dialogues during the masochistic phantasy are pretty frequent. Certain accents or expressions are then deemed very important, the cadence of a certain sentence is tasted voluptuously. . . . In one case a sentence used by the patient's father—"Be careful you don't do it again"—became the content of such a phantasy scene and had to be repeated again and again with a definite melody. The son, who had to be on his knees, would ask with a certain fearful expression, "May I get up?"[12]

This kind of artful structure of fantasy provides the ground for a meeting of intense humiliation and intense pleasure in which the two become one: one's worst humiliation, one's 'exquisite pain,' is also a moment of mystical ecstasy.

Some have argued that the humiliation one feels in masochistic experience is not 'real,' i.e., literal, that it is the very 'unreality' of the pain that makes the experience pleasurable. This argument turns for support to the idea that the masochist has full control over the fantasy or situation. As playwright, director, and leading actor, the 'victim' actually determines the kind, degree, and duration of the humiliation.

The fallacy in this idea is that if there is only an illusion of force, there is also only an illusion of humiliation. In short, humiliation is regarded as unreal because fantasy is regarded as unreal. This attitude could occur only in a culture in which people say, "It's only a fantasy." It fails to understand the vitality and importance of fantasy in human life. It also misses the important fact that most masochists suffer humiliation at having masochistic fantasies at all. Considering the shoddy reputation of masochism, this is as 'real' or 'reality-based' a humiliation as one ever experiences. The shame *at* masochism is the shame *of* masochism: the feeling of having it forced upon one, being subject to it, having little control over its forms, and none at all over its visitation. It is the same sort of shame one feels in being subject to uncontrollable instinctual needs and physiological responses like incontinence, insatiable hunger, ill-timed penile erections, or having to smoke. The need for humiliation, the primary *necessity to experience primal shame*, is itself a humiliating recognition of need.

Masochistic fantasies, enacted or otherwise, satisfy for another reason. People need, and take delight in, fantasy production. Ask the Disneyland folks, who work as much for adults as for children. Or, for an individual example, consider this fantasy of a twenty-nine-year-old woman, who, incidentally, had a stable marriage and a rewarding career. She suffered acutely delicious pangs of shame writing it down, but once she had, she considered telling her husband about it, with an eye to enacting it with him. This is the fantasy:

> My favorite fantasy has me in my living room. It's afternoon. I have made a bet with a man who is a friend, but this man only exists in my fantasy, I don't really know him. We played chess—this is what we bet on—and I lost. The bet was that whoever won could have three wishes filled by the loser: no conditions, except nothing that would cause physical pain. The man comes to the door, I let him in. He says he has come to "collect on the bet." I feel apprehension, but am kind of excited, now that I have to "pay up." (The man is a lot like my husband—not in looks, but he's strong and

quiet and forceful.) In the living room, he says I must do three things for him, as promised, and must not say a word until after the last "wish" is filled. First, he says, I must take all my clothes off. I start to protest this—after all, it's not very private, and I am too embarrassed. He makes a threatening—no, *warning*—gesture and reminds me I lost the bet and agreed to it. (At this point in the fantasy, I begin to feel sexually aroused.) I take my clothes off and stand there naked. He just stares at me, and I feel more and more humiliated and exposed. But it's very exciting too. After awhile, he says the second thing I must do is bring him a glass of wine and serve it to him with both hands, kneeling in front of him. I go to the kitchen. When I come back with the glass, he is sitting at one end of the sofa. This is like a ritual I must perform, and I get more and more sexually excited—being naked, being commanded by him, kneeling, the whole ritual thing just drives me wild, I love it. But I also feel more and more humiliated, more degraded. I know already now in the fantasy we will end up having sex, but I feel humiliated to have to go through all this embarrassment to get there. But since I lost the bet—and that's humiliating too—I have to submit to him. So I kneel and hand him the glass, which he drinks slowly. I feel so scrutinized and ashamed. The third thing he demands is to make love to me. But this part of the fantasy is really past the high point—I'm already so excited I masturbate and have an orgasm quickly. The fantasy just ends in a sort of fade-out.

Though the general motif and circumstances of this fantasy are common enough, its relative richness of detail gives it a specificity we too can scrutinize.

The sense of anticipation is only implied in this written version of the fantasy, but the young woman made it explicit during her analytic sessions. She half-knows what is coming next, that each succeeding demand will be more humiliating and exciting than the preceding. Each element appears integral. There was no conscious plan, though she did deliberately set the opening scene in her living room. Like most people would, she suffered considerable (yet savory) embarrassment in telling her masochistic fantasy, even after it was written down. She had, at best, only partial control over its contents, and none at all over its genesis. Her humiliation is real, however 'contrived' the fantasy situation may be.

The aesthetic and ritualistic character of the fantasy is apparent. The chess game, the 'unveiling,' the kneeling, the serving of the wine, are aesthetically wrought movements and have their own history. They add a religious and aesthetic dimension to the fantasy, besides the sexual one. In psychotherapeutic work, one might work with both the personal and collective factors, moving among plot, feeling, setting, and specific image. This fantasy is rich ground for experiencing and exploring this woman's relationships—including, but certainly not limited to, men and God or gods.

There are a few general statements we can make. It is interesting that there is no physical force exerted—only the bondage of keeping one's word. The absence of punishment also gives this fantasy a particular, individualized twist. The woman has a definite sense of being compelled, forced, but it is to a circumstance—the bet—that she agreed. She has not done anything 'wrong'; she has just lost the game and has to "pay up."

For this woman, humiliation is best and most pleasurably imagined as losing, nakedness, submission-by-paying-up. The fantasy further specifies each of these motifs: losing is a bet to be paid; nakedness is being scrutinized; submission is making an offering, being silent, and kneeling. The motif is particularized in imagery, and each image is refined in specificity. The pleasure lies in the fantasizing and the refinement, and so does much of the humiliation. The fantasy, a relatively autonomous creation of the woman's psyche, is eminently real, as real as her dreams or her breathing or her hunger. The fantasy is the carrier of her feelings of humiliation, shame, pleasure, excitement; it is their image.

Pleasure is constantly refining itself, as we noted before. And sexual pleasure, because it is rooted in the humus of instinctual nature, can bring humility, a sense of lowness, inferiority, inadequacy, shame. This is a different view of things from the traditional psycho-analytic goal, which is to develop gender identity out of the pleasurable, polymorphously perverse, inferior, confused state of in-fantile sexuality. If this goal is reached, one is supposed to feel less inferior, ashamed, and inadequate about sex. Responding to this, Patricia Berry points out that movement out of this confused, shameful state can be a denial of the experience of that confusion and shame. "In fact," she writes, "maybe the inferiority is one of the instinct's very vicissitudes and part of its very pleasure."[13] She suggests keeping inferiority and pleasure together instead of splitting them into polarizations of lust-guilt, id-superego. We are protected from being immobilized or paralyzed by our sexual instincts by knowing at a deep level that we are subject to them, and by ex-periencing that inferiority that is crucial to the knowledge of our primal, lowest level.

> So long as we can feel somewhat sensitive and ashamed about hungry mouths, the anus, clitoris, and penis, about bowels and masturbation—they will not appear as overwhelming powers. Rather, when we are in touch with them, we will also be in touch with a sense of inferiority. Where there is primal sexuality, there is at the same time . . . humility.[14]

To see soul in sex, to see sex as a fantasy of soul, detracts nothing from its animality and the confusions of shame, lowness, and in-feriority. Fantasy helps preserve the animal in us—the hungry wolf, the velvet-eyed doe, the potent bull, the playful kitten—and inhibits that peculiar human pride which has elevated mind over matter, spirit over body, and left us with soul cast adrift, a poignantly lonely species.

A Deflection:
Eros as Sadist

Jung saw in Eros the god of relatedness, who relates by connecting and makes relationship. Unfortunately, Eros suffers some trivialization these days in psychology, in pornography, and in the greeting card industry. In some psychologies, the god has been reduced to 'feeling,' as if the only god were human feeling or his only domain interpersonal relationships. In pornography, the erotic has been reduced to sex; and on Valentine's Day cards, Eros has been reduced to a fat, infantile cherub shooting cartoon arrows.

The authentic Eros is truly a god, a divinity of power, passion, and range. As one of the soul's prime movers, he is capable of cruel as well as compassionate love. In one myth, Eros shoots arrows tipped with lead to poison or frustrate love in his victim. This may mean that love itself can be poisonous and fatal; but it also means that love, for oneself or another, may be experienced as a frustrating cruelty as well as a gentle compassion.

Sometimes in our relatedness we suffer a wounding and tearing apart. This is Eros, too, perhaps what we might call a sadistic Eros. The work of Eros is to love and hate relentlessly, to drive us deeper into relationship with all the parts of ourselves and with others. Sometimes it drives us further still, to relationship with those divinities that rule the soul. The work is a pained and pleasured exposure—in novelist John Fowles's phrase, "love, that need to be naked."[15] Whether we call it submission to an archetypal imperative or submission to the will of God, it remains submission—one of the hallmarks of the masochistic attitude.

Eros, love, relationship, as archetypal forces, are our needs, our emotional instincts. One may simply say that love is needy. On the day of Aphrodite's birth, begins a mythologem,

the gods were making merry, and among them was Metis's son Resource
[Poros], the son of Craft. And when they had supped, Need [Penia] came
begging at the door because there was good cheer inside. Now, it happened
that Resource, having drunk deeply of the heavenly nectar . . . wandered out
into the garden of Zeus and sank into a heavy sleep, and Need, thinking that
to get a child by Resource would mitigate her penury, lay down beside him
and in time was brought to bed of Love [Eros].

The tale continues, drawing these conclusions from the circumstances:

As the son of Resource and Need, it has been his [Eros's] fate to be always
needy; nor is he delicate and lovely as most of us believe, but harsh and arid,
barefoot and homeless, sleeping on the naked earth, in doorways, or in the
very streets beneath the stars of heaven, and always partaking of his
mother's poverty. But, secondly, he brings his father's resourcefulness to his
designs upon the beautiful and good, for he is gallant, impetuous, and
energetic, a mighty hunter, and a master of device and artifice—at once
desirous and full of wisdom, a lifelong seeker after truth, an adept in sorcery,
enchantment, and seduction.[16]

So Eros is tough, with purposes and a mind of his own. From his
mother, he inherits the quality of being driven by need, and thus
driving us, like a sadist. A driving force himself, he may use force to
drive his way into our lives. So we feel, and are, driven by love and
desire—sometimes sleepless, starving, obsessed. So too do we find
ourselves unable *not* to relate to the objects of our passions—despite
our best laid plans, the timeless wisdom of restraint, and good advice
from those who know better. We can see Resource, the father of
Eros, sometimes in Eros too, for we often must wonder at the com-
binations of lovers and friends, and at the ingenuity and craftsmanship with which relationships are forged and maintained.

The inner sadist can be any complex, quality, image—any part of
psyche—that is trying to come through to consciousness, make itself
heard, find living space, win attention, even in its torturing

unloveliness. Often we have to be dragged, whipped, beaten into psychic change. We often experience this thrust as sadistic, a cruel demand, because something in ego-consciousness is being driven or forced to change. Intrapsychically, masochistic submission is a movement of submission of one psychic part to another, one image to another, entailing all the emotions attached to this experience: fear, love, hate, disgust, fascination, humiliation.

Eros, the beautiful winged god of Love and Desire, loves devotedly and torments with desire. Simone Weil has said that all love is sadistic because it is possessive. But it is also true that love, when it reaches that rare place that is not possessive, has strong masochistic components; it longs to serve, to submit, to lay pride and power at the feet of another, to abandon itself nakedly, sexually, emotionally, physically, to another's will. Love is bondage; the lover is a slave. When one loves deeply, passionately, totally, submission to that love is not only a degradation but also an ecstasy.

CHAPTER 4

Mortification, or Alchemical Masochism

> *His flaw'd heart—*
> *Alack! too weak the conflict to support;*
> *'Twixt two extremes of passion, joy and*
> *grief,*
> *Burst smilingly.*
>
> SHAKESPEARE, *King Lear*

> *If my man beats me*
> *robs me blind . . .*
> *long as he don't leave me*
> *I don't mind.*
> *I would beg and I would crawl*
> *though it does no good at all . . .*
> *the head says No*
> *and the heart says*
> *Go down on your knees, woman*
> *and keep on holding on.*
>
> JANIS IAN, "You've Got Me On A String"

The alchemical art provides a rich contextual pattern in which to place masochism in psychic work. The alchemical laboratory, like the analyst's consulting room, is an imaginal place where there is no rigid distinction between science and art, no arbitrary separation of object and subject, no schizophrenic splits between psyche and matter. Alchemical psychology seems to have a better understanding of masochism than psychiatry's explanations and pornography's illustrations, and gives us a better word for it: *mortificatio*—the operation of mortification. Alchemy accurately perceives the compelling necessity of this operation as one part in a series of the complete alchemical or individuation process. Not all of what we call masochism today can be subsumed under mortification; but the alchemical operation leads us back to an essence, an archetypal, psychological experience.

Perhaps the strongest advantage of an alchemical context is that it allows us to see masochism as a *subtle* (literally, "finely woven" in Latin) experience. Both psychiatry and pornography tend to emphasize the obvious, the gross manifestations of masochism in its pathology and its literal sexualism. But alchemical psychology is concerned with the subtle body of psyche, its intangible reality, its genuine but invisible substance. After all, most of our masochistic experiences are not obvious or gross. We are not literally whipped or handcuffed, but we take pleasure sometimes in being hurt, cuffed, or wounded. The barbed word, the stinging inflection, the cutting gesture—each strikes the subtle body of soul, and somewhere in the deep recesses of secret being, we know it is oddly stimulating and not always unpleasant. The experience is no less real for lack of chains; indeed, the more subtle the experience, the more we may feel its psychic reality, without misleading exaggeration or literalism. In the same manner, psychically-based masochism is no escape from materiality. As in any process in alchemy, the concrete, actual *body* of the operation moves simultaneously with the subtle soul-process. We live our mortification in body and soul together.

Alchemy sees all its operations as necessary, and each operation is a mode of therapy. "Dissolution," "coagulation," "distillation," "conjunction," "separation," "fixation," "putrefaction," to name only a few operations, comprise a sort of soul technology, a technique of psychotherapy. They provide a metaphorical base for understanding psychic experiences. In psychology today, some terms from alchemy have been retained, e.g., *fixation, sublimation, projection*. And the conditions the alchemical terms describe have been retained in popular speech: "getting it together" *(coniunctio),* "breaking down" and "falling apart" (*dissolutio, separatio*), "feeling rotten" (*putrefactio*), "being in a fix" (*fixatio*).

As its Latin root (*mors*) shows, mortification is connected with death, with a movement to a psychological perspective where life is no longer encrusted with superfluities and literalism. *Mortificatio* is a death-making operation, moving away from surface appearances, deeper into the underworld of "shades," of psychic essences. All our dyings, in night dreams and day calamities, are experiences of death; all our mortifications are experiences of soul-making.

In *mortificatio*, the *prima materia*—our primary psychic material, whatever is the matter with us—is worked over. "Beating up on oneself" can be a beating, a pounding and preparing of a piece of psychic food. Salisbury steak, for example, requires that the meat be beaten to tenderize, soften, and make it more absorbent. A food blender is a modern alchemical vessel (a "masochizer"[1]), tormenting what is put into it by cutting, chopping, grinding, whipping.

The Greeks thought that the seeds put into a medicinal mortar mixture were living seeds, which were tortured, beaten, and crushed in the mortar—masochized into medicine. Here we can speak of being masochized instead of being masochists. It is something that happens to us rather than something we are. We undergo the operation of *mortificatio* when we are absorbed in self-blame, self-attack, being hard on ourselves, giving ourselves no mercy, no quarter. It is as if our souls in their mortification cry out for condemnation, hard penance, death. There is a kind of abrasive, abusive, sadistic grinding going on in psyche, and we feel tortured, whipped, crushed, weighted down.

There are times when one is simply but emphatically *not* okay. As homeopathic medicine knows, the remedy is not necessarily to introduce an opposite. Alchemical thinking is in likenesses as well as oppositions. The antidote to humiliation is not pride, or a reassertion of one's self-respect or virtues or positive qualities. It is humility. There are occasions of fault, failure, exposures of shameful weakness, which can be borne only by yielding completely to the feeling of them. Mortification is a heavy reminder that the matter is *not* all right. At such times, feeling bad is better handled by feeling worse: if we sink to the deathly bottom, the pit, we may die to shame as well as of it.

The operation of *mortificatio* produces a condition known in religious language as contrition. ("Contrition" is derived from the Latin *tero*, meaning "to grind.") When we have to apologize for a serious offense, we do not want to be patted on the head and told how right it all is when we know it is all wrong. We need our offenses and our feelings about them realized and affirmed, not cursorily excused, for this is an appropriately serious affirmation of our soul's suffering and our human limitation. Easy sympathy trivializes the mortification. Mortification is a death experience filled with shame; our souls will not tolerate a casual atonement.

Mortificatio is a psychological operation, not a moral one. It is neither good nor bad, better nor worse. It is a necessary, just-so operation. As we recall that *mortificatio* is a death-making and deliteralizing operation, it becomes clear that the operation is necessary, not for moral ego-strengthening, but for realization of hard psychic reality. This operation involves us in a deeper kind of 'Reality Therapy.' We cringe to realize the place in psyche which is beyond ego-control, especially in its ugliness or banality. It is a hard thing, hard to take. "How many there be who search out . . . but yet cannot endure the torments."[2]

Fainting is one bodily manifestation of a death experience, a dramatic, sudden, and mortifying descent into the black realm of the dead. In a faint, one is lost in deathlike oblivion, at the borderline in a condition where there is pulsing life without ego-consciousness. Once reawakened, one's ego is reminded, to its shame, that it has been entirely at the mercy of the body, its balance and resistance abruptly seized.

Blushing is another mortification in the body, a hot body flash, a painfully obvious signal of dying of shame. It is an alchemical operation producing a state of redness. Blushing is not only skin deep. Its redness signifies rawness and acute sensitivity. It is the raw meat of the matter, whether in our kitchens, the alchemical laboratory, or in our souls. Blushing is another of those physiological phenomena against which will-power is of no avail. That sudden hot red flush cannot be stopped, nor can the automatic gesture of covering one's face, the uncontrollable urge to hide. Blushing itself mortifies, and mortification is visible in the blush.

In his 1839 essay on "The Physiology or Mechanism of Blushing," Thomas Burgess, member of the Royal College of Surgeons, declared that "blushing may be styled the poetry of the Soul," and that "blushing is the lava of the heart produced by an eruption of feeling."[3] Not surprisingly, Burgess calls blushing one of the four "humanizing creativities" (the other three being creativities of the reproductive organs, of pregnancy, and of digestion). He concludes: "The irrepressible blush . . . clearly demonstrates the impossibility of the *will* ever being able to overcome or control the *genuine* emotions of the Soul."[4] The remembrance of bitterness, shame, mortification brings the experience again to the cheek's surface, as a wound and a soul-poem both. Shame has a long memory, and it burns.

Mortification is an a priori condition of human existence. The soul is already tortured, psyche's twistedness a given. The operation of mortification is not a quantitative technique (add torture, subtract torture), but a *quality* of soul. It is another ego heroism to think we might eliminate our mortifications or clear up our complexes. A complex, as James Hillman once described it, is "a twisted organization of psychic elements, a group of ideas twisted together in a special way, held together by an emotional archetypal core: a wreath, a constellation of intertwined motifs.''' A complicated, complex personality is twisted and tortured, yet bears its extremities in a finely-wrought intricacy of distinct and distinctive emotions, images, memories, gestures.

When we think alchemically, psychologically, we contradict a common prejudice about psychotherapy. Its purpose is not to straighten out, untwist, untorture so that we feel no pain. Straightening out is something one does to curly hair, juvenile delinquents, and traffic snarls, not necessarily to one's soul. If it is truly depth therapy, an attending to soul, we ought to get more complicated, more complex, more mortified. Soul-work includes the confusion and inner realization that we are inextricably bound to our complexes, our unconsciousness, our animality, and our mortality. Therapy ought to move us not *just* to our 'inner' selves, but also to a sense that external events also have interior significance that can be perceived with the 'third eye'—including, and maybe especially, symptoms and daily aches and pains and the thousand natural shocks that flesh is heir to. Therapy is to realize more soul, including its torturedness, to understand its nature and to attend to its care. Perhaps therapy would be more effective if we tried less to *eliminate* torture and more to *endure* it.

Paradoxically, it is sometimes by enduring the torments that change comes about. This is perhaps what Jesus meant when he said that by losing one's life, one finds it. Sometimes it is only by suffering a death of submission that one can stand under and understand what is necessary in our souls. There are no guarantees. Genuine submission excludes a bribing attitude—that the submission will buy rewards—for that is no true submission.

After one analysand's long, painful time in analysis, her masochistic complex emerged in personified form. She then gave this psychic person a name, which signaled her realization that the

complex was not a 'thing,' but a living being with intentions and
needs of its own. In effect, a new vessel was created to carry this partial personality, who could then be engaged in imaginative dialogue.
Analysand-as-ego and analysand-as-masochist met to experience a
new reality. In one active imagination, this is part of the exchange
that took place:

Jane (ego)	Maybe I am just up to my old tricks of trying to ward you off with my over-sensitivity, but, I mean, you don't seem to mind hurting me. You feel hostile to me.
Janice (masochist)	Well, I'm trying to crawl up out of the mire too. Your extreme ambivalence toward me has been shit to live with. Of course, I tend to take a lot of shit from everyone, and it's not all unpleasant.
Jane	So you know that I've always secretly cherished you.
Janice	Oh yes. And secrets are so intimate. . . . I need you most of all. It wouldn't be right with others if it weren't right with you.
Jane	Oh Janice, you are very smart to know that.
Janice	I've done a lot of thinking, flat on my back.
Jane	You are elemental.
Janice	Oh come now. You are trying to smooth things over. I know you still hate me.
Jane	You still want to be hated by me, don't you? . . .
Janice	I want you to have a basic love for me. I want you to realize me. . . .
Jane	But I'm talking about your getting off on being despised.
Janice	The worst thing is no attention. Positive attention bestows an obligation. Negative attention is intense and important and awesome. A beating can have the rhythm of lovemaking. If you don't deserve anything, everything is a gift.

Jane	What you've said is heavy and will have to seep in. But don't you think you deserve *anything*?
Janice	Oh, I hate to talk about justice! I deserve to be realized.

•

The mortifying deaths one suffers have purposes, if we can find them. There are meanings in masochistic experiences, things to be learned, necessities to be met. Franz Kafka wrote, "One learns when one has to; one learns when one needs a way out; one learns at all costs. One stands over oneself with a whip; one flays oneself at the slightest opposition.''[6] In masochism, one accepts—even welcomes—one's pain, not because of superficial pleasure, but because of deep necessity.

Mortificatio is an operation of torture to re-shape, re-mold, re-form something—a metal, a substance, a psychological complex—so that the soul can be redeemed from the *massa confusa* of literalisms, one-sided identifications and dominance of the ego. But it is a redemption through torturous knowledge—*gnosis*—and through *psychopathology* ("the suffering of meaning") rather than through divine forgiveness.

> The psyche would not be loved out of its pathology, nor forgiven. Grace, yes, and *caritas*, send down what you will, but do not forgive me the means by which the divine powers connect and become real: my complexes, which are my sacrifices to these powers. Until I sense them in my confusions, the Gods remain abstract and unreal. Forgiveness of the confusions in which I am submerged, the wounds that give me eyes to see with, the errant and renegade in my behavior, blots out the Gods' main route of access.[7]

The care and cultivation we give to the process of *mortificatio*, the hovering over small mortifying wounds, the salting of shameful memories, the private blush of perverse desire—all these have their place in our souls and in the art of masochism.

Every mortification feels like a death in the soul. Sometimes we have a sense of anticipation, however vague or subliminal, a half-certain awareness that we have been placed on this path of death, and it is useless to resist it. In masochism, non-resistance becomes submission; and submission to death—indeed, complicity with it—leads to the idea of masochism as metaphorical suicide.

Psychoanalytic theory holds that suicide is ultimate masochism. It sees masochism as hostility turned inward or upon oneself as victim, suicide as the final act of sadism against oneself. In this view, masochism is primarily an ego phenomenon, one's death flung in the face of the gods as the only victory in one's life. This understanding of masochism misses the paradox in both masochism and death, and the soul's love and suffering of paradox. If we focus only upon the literal death which is entailed in suicide, we lose the sense of death as a way of seeing the psychic aspect or essence of what is going on in our lives. The dead who dwelt in the Greek mythic underworld of Hades were thought to be "shades," from whom all the encrustations and superfluities of literal life, and all the clutter of waking consciousness, were peeled away so that only a quintessence remained. Our everyday consciousness usually is opposed and resistant to this way of seeing essence, this death-perspective. But deep within the soul, in hidden invisible currents, there is a movement toward death, toward depth, toward essence. It may be that this movement is more obvious in masochists. Masochism itself seems to be an effort to keep the paradox, to preserve the sense of resisting and yet consenting to death at the same time.

A middle-aged woman brought to a therapy session a dream which spoke in precisely these paradoxical terms. This woman had a long history of masochistic experience, both sexual and religious, and at the time she had the dream was entangled in several major life crises. This was her dream:

> I'm walking with an older friend, Kate, and I think another friend, Dick, is with us. There is a large mausoleum with a family section of tombs. A large slab marked with a family name, "Thomas," is on the wall, and below it is a smaller slab inscribed "aidos."[8] I'm apparently a family member, to be buried in the stone tomb marked "aidos," as if this is my name even though it sounds strange and foreign to me. Kate is going to give me a drug injection which will "put me to sleep" or "put me to death." I am very willing, perhaps even asked for it. I am drawn to death with a longing to rest forever, out of troublesome life, and to be at peace. But as we come closer to the moment, I get panicky and terrified, filled with desire to live, to not miss anything no matter how painful. I want to be dead and I want to live, both at the same time. At the last minute I pull back, desperately unable to decide, unable to go through with it.

With Hamlet, the dreamer faces the timeless question, to be or not to be. Our dreamer is not literally suicidal. The dream, speaking its metaphorical language, shows her desiring and resisting death as a radical change in life attitude. On the one hand, she is willing—asking—to see life from the perspective of death, from a deeper level where her life crises have meaning for her soul. Yet she also resists, gets panicky and terrified at the sight/site of her burial place. Ay, there's the rub. She is caught in ambivalence, caught in paradox, caught at a point between life and death. Awake, her life is a shame; asleep, her death is a shame. It is in the place of the goddess Aidos, or Shame, where the dreamer is to be buried, initiated into the mystery of death. In her shame and mortification is also holy reverence, a work of death (mortificatio) for the sake of soul. Her redemption might come through hard, tombstone-like mortification, a deeper realization of shameful wounds.

The operation of *mortificatio*, or psychological masochism, is not pathological in itself. On the contrary, it is a means by which we can see, through experience, our hidden, crushing pathologies. Masochism becomes pathological when it is literalized and when its machinations block, instead of lead into, self-revelation and self-knowledge. When we are fixated too long and too completely—wholly identified—it can become the *only* way we see ourselves. When literalization and exclusive identification happen, we are stuck in the mortar which is the mixed ingredients of our life: as the suffering hero, the rejected lover, the hairshirted ascetic, the misunderstood rebel, the unappreciated martyr, the sufferer-on-automatic. We are ejected up, out of a deep-seated suffering onto a superficial plane of appearances, of apparent suffering: the fantasy of martyrdom.

A Deflection:
The Contract as Sadist

The ordinary and legal purpose of a contract is to ensure fairness of treatment among contracting parties, so that each receives just consideration. But the purpose of a masochistic contract is to ensure unfairness. A masochistic contract guarantees an unequal relationship, in which one party has all the overt power, and the other party, none. The contract is a fantasy of contracting the masochist, shrinking him, making him small.

Sometimes a masochistic contract is overt, as one finds in Masoch's *Venus in Furs*; sometimes it is implied, as in the woman's fantasy of the lost bet at chess (Chapter 3) and in many enacted sexual fantasies. The contract outlines the terms of the fantasy: partners are assigned roles, conditions are specified, penalties are described, and a time limitation is set. Here, the contract itself governs both partners, acting as master to whom both the masochist and his partner must submit.

While many fantasies have elements as fixed as the terms of a contract, in masochistic contracts the sequence of events truly becomes a chain, manacling the masochist not only to the psychic necessity of feeling what the fantasy presents, but also to each inescapable link of specific movement, word, condition, and most of all, penalty. The fantasy-contract, born of a passionate need for submission, humiliation, pain, and defeat, forges each link—hard, strong, and unbending as the masochist is soft, weak, and bowed. Form and style are thoroughly imprisoned in content. Each "whereas" slams like an iron door; each "therefore" strikes like a rawhide whip.

The idea of "contractual masochism" is rooted in the archetypal image of fateful boundaries. The strict terms of a masochistic contract serve two purposes. First, they are boundaries, marking the fantasy *as fantasy*, limiting it so that it does not spill over into literal role identifications. In carrying out the instincts in soul, fantasies strive for attention and enactment. But it is also true, as Freud said, that instincts carry their own inhibitions. Physical enactment of a masochistic fantasy gives a shape and body to the fantasy, while the contract holds it firmly within bounds of the imaginal world. This interplay between imagination and enactment preserves and augments a sense of ritual and depth.

Second, the contract heightens the limitations, the bondage, the punishment by giving them specificity. These contractual terms become binding because they are bound themselves. Fixed by the fantasy itself, these contractual terms do not refer to any a priori constructs of justice or morality except those which are intrinsic to the fantasy. Like Fate, they convey the sense of immutability. Once set, the terms become the cruel, oppressive masters to whom one is in bondage.

Paradoxically, the fateful immutability of terms and their fixation in time are precisely the features that place the masochist in the mythic realm of timeless soul, the eternal nowhere-everywhere of dreams, death, psychosis. Fleeting, tortured moments of scorching shame are, at the same time, merciless eternities. Once shame has moved into memory, its experience is fixed timelessly, implacably, mortared in humiliation, cast in masochistic remembrance, a permanent monument. It must be observed, served, ritually revisited with pain and nostalgia. It exacts a somber, more-than-personal due, like Memorial Day services. A shameful experience forces us to remember not just our personal pain and inadequacy, but also that impersonal archetypal ground where there is no individuality.

Fixing limitations, or laws, as a contract does, necessitates penalties for transgressing them. But the guilt incurred by transgression of fateful boundaries goes beyond personal ego-guilt. Specifically, such transgression evokes that archetypal—also existential—sense of wrongness which consists, on the one hand, of humiliation at being *human*, and on the other, of presumptuousness at being in too-close affinity with the divine. Either stance is a sin for which eternal atonement must be made. It is a guilt of *being* rather than *doing*. As in the Christian story of original sin, as in Dionysian initiation rites, as in the story of Prometheus, it is a necessary guilt, or guilt of Necessity, for it gives definition and boundaries to humanness.

Simone Weil said that it is an inescapable fact of human nature that the feeling of guilt, at its center, is identical with the feeling of being *I*. Like those of all creatures, the terms of our lives are set by time, gravity, biochemistry, genetics, family, society, species, country, and a host of other factors. Our births and deaths are binding, our natures given. These terms contract us, shrink us; sometimes they feel as strict, as unfair, as cruel, as the acts of a sadist. But the contract is fixed and necessary. Its terms force our humanity down upon us, offering us, as we become the offerings, the agonized and vital experience of human being.

CHAPTER 5

Martyrdom, or The Mania of Misery

Thou hast not half the power to do me harm
As I have to be hurt.
                SHAKESPEARE, *Othello*

Well, I lay my head on the railroad track
Waiting on the Double "E"
But the train don't run by here no more
Poor poor pitiful me.
                LINDA RONSTADT, "Poor Poor Pitiful Me"

Masochists are witnesses to soul; martyrs are victims. Freud thought that religion, among other things, was a neurosis; but it is probably truer that neurosis is a religion. One makes a religion of one's neurosis—which is one reason it is so difficult to effect a conversion, that is, to change it. If masochism has a religious attitude toward suffering, then martyrdom has a neurotic one.

The dictionary states that a martyr is "one who willingly suffers death rather than renounce his religion; one who is put to death or endures great suffering on behalf of any belief, principle, or cause; one who undergoes severe or constant suffering; a person who seeks sympathy and attention by pretending to or exaggerating pain, deprivation, etc."[1]

There is nothing in these definitions of "martyr" concerning either humiliation or pleasure, those two essential ingredients of masochism. With the exception of the dictionary's last phrase, these definitions call forth images from early Christianity—the rending of flesh by lions in the Roman Coliseum, the broken limbs of St. Catherine on her wheel, the arrow-pierced body of St. Sebastian, and the charred remains of St. Lawrence on his iron grill. What comes to us from these images is not the stench of blood and burned flesh, but the "odor of sanctity." And the last definition—a person who seeks sympathy and attention by pretending to or exaggerating pain, deprivation, etc.—conveys not the odor of sanctity but the stink of neurosis: one sniffs out pretense, exaggeration, and the endless, repetitious justifications of one's imposed sufferings.

Martyrdom is not a denominational or sectarian phenomenon. We all have a bit of martyr in us. A secular version of the modern martyr appears vividly in certain types of neglected spouses; in people who parade one disastrous love affair after another; in the stereotype of the tyrannically weak mother and mother-in-law; in overworked men and women who insist that they are *sacrificing* their entire lives for the sake of the company, their jobs, their clients, their children or families. One hears the voice of martyrdom in loud angry cries of complaint ("You give me nothing but trouble!") and in pitiful little whimpers ("You don't pay any attention to me."). It can skewer victims on its hot blade of imposed suffering or prickle in tiny accumulations, radiating a subtle but gathering uneasiness.

Because it is an externalization, lacking inner depth, martyrdom cannot be fully satisfying in itself. Martyrdom lacks the careful observation and containment of fantasy in an alchemical vessel; since the 'source' of suffering is projected out everywhere, it lacks the subtlety, nuance, and differentiation of suffering found in psychological (non-literal) masochism.

Our wounded egos put us in the martyr fantasy. Martyrs tend to see their situation simply: their suffering has been unjustly imposed on them by persons and forces from the outside. This superficiality of self-pity blocks genuine compassion. Their attitude is self-righteous and self-centered. Only through heroic tolerance and false humility do they feel able to bear up under the mysteriously unfair things that keep happening.

Martyrs do not accept the experience of suffering. They actually avoid it by using their apparent victimization as ego ammunition. Martyrs are too proud of their suffering, too manipulative about their righteousness, to suffer humiliation. Thus martyrs are possessed by literalisms and projections. Their suffering finds its primary meaning as proof of their victimization. This is an oppressively empty view, one that lacks metaphorical resonance and a sense of intrapsychic reality. However, it is just this absence of vitalizing humiliation, this lack of contact with the inner soul, that may eventually press psyche to a deeper ground, where suffering leads to humiliation, and genuine humility can be born of suffering.

I recall one patient of mine as an example of this movement from martyrdom to masochism. Divorced, unemployed, mother of two children, she came into analysis at age thirty-six. She spent the first six months reciting a litany of complaints. She suffered from headache and backache (heartache didn't come until later). She suffered from an ex-husband who would not meet her demands, from thankless children who needed too much, and from a lover who didn't appreciate her. She suffered every 'injustice' society could inflict as a victim of the welfare office, the unemployment office, and the economic social system. Even her dreams looked to her like affirmations of her rightness. When I frequently failed to support or encourage her martyrdom, I too joined the growing list of villains. She very nearly drowned in self-pity.

Then one day she brought a dream in which her mother-in-law starred in the role of 'martyr.' In the dream, the mother-in-law was complaining, loudly and obnoxiously, to the dreamer. The dreamer flew into a rage and yelled, "Stop playing the martyr!" For the first time, my patient really woke up and heard herself; she told me her dream mother-in-law was complaining about exactly the things she herself had—and so she heard herself in her own dream. It was a confession, a painful recognition, and a humiliating acknowledgment that she had been the martyr all along.

That dream and that acknowledgment did not solve her problems, but they did enable her to begin moving out of the martyr fantasy into a deeper—and more masochistic—experience. She began to suffer in a more opened way, accepting the pain and pleasure of submission to humiliating limitations, self-deceptions, childishness, and helplessness. Slowly, a genuine compassion for her own pain and grief emerged, and some wisdom, a more subtle sense of humor, a strange pleasure of discovery, and the beginning of healing.

*

The movement from martyrdom to masochism is also a movement from guilt to shame. Guilt and shame can be defined and delineated conceptually, but experientially their boundaries are very difficult to discern.

Guilt begins with law; shame begins with realization of a greater-than-ego Self. The vocabulary of guilt operates in terms of right and wrong, crime and punishment, culpability and rectification. Doing wrong implies the possibility of doing right; guilt implies the possibility of rectification, of righting the wrong, as an act of will. Thus guilt lies within the sphere of the ego, inflating it with both an excess of fault and excess of power to rectify. Often a pathologically guilty ego covers an inflated ego. It is not always easy to see the power driving through our guilt. But sometimes in a sudden flash of self-reflection, or in a guilty glance at another, we reach back to our premises. Then the assumption may emerge with shocking clarity: ''Everything I touch turns to shit'' is a mirror-image of ''Everything I touch turns to gold.''

Martyrs are incessantly guilty. Probably their most common refrain is "Why me?" or "What did I do to deserve this?" Yet these are rarely sincere questions, for at the same time, the martyr denies this guilt, projecting it onto others: "*You* make me feel guilty!" or "If only *he* could see what *he* is doing to me!"

From the facade of these questions, and from the aura of 'weakness' which surrounds the martyr, one might expect him to be a pushover. Yet any real confrontation brings out his true posture. Step beyond sympathy or agreement, and up he leaps, a hero or anti-hero, ready to engage in full-scale defensive battle. The spoils are the (dubious) laurels of who is the most guilty or the most victimized.

An approach that works through ego, in therapy or other relationship, can be helpful, but only to a point: such an approach engages ego in battle, alternately forcing the martyr to his knees to face his real sins and desires, then hauling him to his feet again to learn to defend himself in 'honest' combat. He finishes bloodied, but unbowed. This approach is active and may change behavior—but it does not necessarily change vision. In one sense, it tries to cure the martyr's persecution complex by forcing the ego to fight back—a defensive stance that usually increases the sense of persecution.

Slipping through the vicious cycle—the unresolvable debate about who is victim and who is guilty, how one is lying and how to fight 'right'—one must try to reach to the figure inside the knight's armor, to the paradoxical truth of his being.

A deeper antidote to guilt lies not in rectification or even forgiveness—but in perceiving the archetypal patterns in which one is caught. The question becomes, "Who is it in me, what archetype is moving me in this direction or that, informing my view of things?"

Theorists have given much attention to guilt in masochism, linking it quite naturally with punishment. Masochism then takes on a *legal* cast, its rules and penalties outlined in a masochistic 'contract.' But this masochistic contract is also a fantasy of contracting, shrinking, being reduced. The pathologically guilty, inflated ego ("I caused all this!") is a denial of the contracted ego that is submissive to shame. It is not the martyr's guilt, but the masochist's shame which goes beyond what one *does* to what one *is*. Thus the shame in masochism keeps alive the sense of psychological and religious purpose.

Shame belongs to the dimension of soul and implies the non-existence of antidote, the permanence of deficiency, the impossibility of rectification (and also of justification). It is the sense of permanent lack, insufficiency, inadequacy which cannot be made right or corrected by any activity of the ego. No amount of will power or prayer or even suffering will do the trick. In its very nature, its 'natural state,' the soul is never complete, and the more complete it is, the more its lacunae become obvious. The experience of the soul's incompleteness and darkness is precisely the experience of shame. Guilt is a moral and legal category; shame belongs to the religious experience of psyche.

*

There is no need to drop the religious association with the martyr as one who "willingly suffers death rather than renounce his religion." We need here only replace religion with the idea of neurosis to recognize the psychological martyr: one who willingly suffers the death of his soul rather than renounce his neurosis. If, with Jung, we imagine a neurosis to be a one-sided attitude, then neurosis is a false narrowness, like a person with two good eyes who wears blinders. Those things that could widen his vision—the peripheral, the nuances, the new angles—are unseen. A neurosis is not as much blindness as a limited vision whose limitation is not perceived. It works for, or serves, the ego attitude. It constricts at the same time that it protects the ego attitude, like a wall that keeps people both out and in. A neurosis imprisons the soul to preserve one-sidedness. And it always works—that's why it hangs on for so long.

The suffering of the psychological martyr has, in large measure, little meaning because the *source* of the martyr's suffering is perceived as coming from outside—from 'the environment,' from a non-sympathetic spouse or friend, from the Internal Revenue Service, from ungrateful children. The source of discomfort is projected: "other people make me suffer." This misperception discourages self-knowledge. This is not to say that there is no such thing as legitimate suffering and hardship from outside forces. Life brings all manner of vicissitudes and struggles, sometimes by special delivery. None are entirely of our own making. The difference for soul has to do with one's psychological attitude toward that suffering. The martyr's attitude is marked by complaint and self-justification rather than devotion and valuing, by self-pity rather than self-compassion, by generalized feelings of helplessness rather than a true recognition of specific limitations. Breast-beating, yes, but no true *mea culpa* for the martyr!

Martyrdom lacks depth. A martyr's suffering is neither conscious nor instructive; more accurately, martyrdom is just boring, to those who are his listeners and victims, and eventually to the martyr himself. Martyrdom is a refrain sung again and again without harmony and with little variation. Although, psychologically, the martyr digests little, he needs some nourishment, a few fresh sources of torment to satisfy the fantasy. The martyr moves on a horizontal level, looking about here and there in search of a source worthy to make him suffer. In contrast, the masochist struggles (with varying degrees of unsuccess)—kicks and screams against the downward pull—while still letting go and falling. The ground to which he falls is solid, the humus of which he is made, his substance. While it breaks him down, it also breaks his fall. The blacker it is, the richer it is, like fertile earth. In this damp humiliation of descent, the masochist may be close to a new insight, a fresh image, a new green possibility, a potential change.

Two dreams from a woman in her early thirties serve as illustration. A deeply religious woman, she had a deeply disturbing masochistic complex lodged like a giant thorn in the base of her psyche. She could see no value or purpose at all in her ''perverse'' desire for psychic pain. After several years of struggling, in and out of analysis, she had this dream:

> I am being driven in the back seat of a car, seated between two friends, David and Ann. By some sort of trick David gets a pair of handcuffs on me with Ann helping him. I get panicky and struggle, but David is stronger and he hooks the handcuffs to a hook in the car ceiling, and that has a separate lock. I have to ride on my knees on the floor with my arms up and head bowed. I feel completely defeated and humiliated. They are taking me to prison. I feel guilty and terrified and betrayed. No one speaks to me. After a long time David puts a key in my hand. I am startled and have a fleeting thought that they will now let me go. But David says, ''It won't do you any good.'' I soon see why: I can release myself from the ceiling hook, but I am still handcuffed. They will not make room for me on the seat, so I have to stay on the floor on my knees. Then David gives me a box with the key to the handcuffs. But when I open it, there are dozens of little odd metal pieces. I have to put the key together. We get closer to the prison, while I fumble desperately in a panic for the key. In despair, I turn on my knees and bury my head in my hands on the seat. I can't take any more.

Upon waking, this woman felt it was the ''worst dream''[1] of her life, the worst thing she could imagine. She found it an intolerable image to see and feel herself so bound and hooked and helpless. With deep reluctance, she admitted to something like a ''thrill'' at the same time, for she felt a peculiar satisfaction in seeing the worst.

Intuitively, she sensed that having hit bottom, a change in the complex was beginning. Less than two weeks later, she had this dream:

> I'm in a huge temple. I am insane, with some kind of religious insanity. There is an elite temple group of 120 boys who do secret things. I want to get into that group, but it is a capital crime to know the secrets. I have two friends who try to help me in my wild insanity. Outside the door of the secret group's room, the young man pushes gently and whispers to me, "Get down on your knees." I feel deep rebellion against this humiliating position, but once down I become immobile. I am supposed to be praying, but I am watching through the keyhole, entranced. The leader of the group announces something about a "hidden treasure." At this climax I am glued to the keyhole, straining to see and hear everything. Someone opens the outer door and we are seen. My friends drag me away from the keyhole. But when we walk into the main sanctuary (the whole congregation is there) I do so with great dignity and composure, lost in thought. Someone in the congregation asks me a question. I say very quietly, still in a semi-trance, "I have found the treasure." This statement has an almost magical effect: everyone turns to me, makes way for me to walk. It is as if a spell has been broken, the secret has been an oppressive one, and now the congregation need not be afraid. They are awed at me, I am awed at the secret of the treasure. I was prepared for them to punish me because I committed the worst crime. But I am welcomed, and someone suggests we all sing a hymn.

In both dreams, the woman is humiliated to be on her knees. In the first dream she is victimized—driven, struggling, chained, and hooked—between two friends who seem more like enemies. Like a martyr, she is not aware of anything 'wrong' that she has done, yet a 'punishment' falls mysteriously and torturously from the outside. As in guilt, the emphasis is on *doing*: what she has *done*, a frenzy of action, using a key, putting another one together, fumbling and finally despairing, unable to act. It is almost as if all the action itself has hooked her in a psychic paralysis. The second dream portrays the woman as insane and holy. Her friends appear truly 'friendly' throughout, and one *gently* pushes her to her knees; she goes down more willingly this time, and once down, she stays because she is *en-tranced*—entered into, led into an entrance, perhaps initiated.

In the first dream, there was a key in pieces with no keyhole; in the second, there was a keyhole with no key. In the second dream, by submitting to the humiliation and danger, she *becomes* the key, in effect, by looking through the keyhole—a key move which gives her a new perspective. What to *do* is no problem—her 'doing' is one with her essence. Once she is in proper position, she has become a key figure, visionary, one who is revealed, possessed of a treasure. It is not her action but her being which inspires awe, bringing release to the congregation.

More important for our purposes than interpretation is the effect these dreams had. It is as if this woman's psychic center of gravity was moved lower, to the ground. She moved, in fact, far down enough to reach an awe-full psychic state below guilt where there is no punishment. It was her own 'insane,' perverse perception, her way of seeing through to the mystery. For the first time the dreamer was able to see purpose in her masochism. The dreams portrayed this paradox—to be humiliated and entranced—as a state of being, or a mode of consciousness. For her, masochism was a way of seeing into her insanity, and through it to the "treasure." She moved from the sense of a prison, a place of guilt and punishment, to a religious temple, a place of deep soul riches.

Yet it is also criminal, sneaky, shameful, this unnatural manner of discovery, this snooping from the knees that looks like kneeling in prayer. Even her manner of learning is suspect. She is tricked into a masochistic posture from outside forces in the first dream, and tricked into learning its value for herself in the second. Though we may see the second dream as a completion of the first, it would be misleading to suggest that they show any simple progressive movement. Through these dreams the woman recognized that the means and the end cannot be separated. There is redemption *in* the terrible

humiliation, not just in spite of or after it. The discovery of treasure
does not change or mitigate the sordid, inglorious, humiliating
business of getting there; indeed, this realization is part of the
treasure. The sense of paradox is essential to masochism. She is in
bondage to her masochism and in thrall to it at the same time; carrying her desire and resistance, she feels it as both intolerable wound
and inestimable wealth.

*

Sometimes people go to frightening lengths to avoid humiliation.
The martyr fantasy needs a touch of paranoia to keep it alive on the
one hand, and to keep it from changing on the other. Without the
stimulus of the paranoid fantasy, the martyr becomes depressed in a
way foreign to him. This depression can signal the need to be
pressed down inside rather than to be searching outside for sources
of persecution. But the usual reaction is to retreat into paranoia as
refuge from unwelcome, humiliating consciousness. The advantage
of a paranoid sense of attack for the martyr is that it relieves or lifts,
if not eliminates, his depression.

Avoidance, like denial, is one classical defense mechanism
recognized by psychoanalysis. When it comes to humiliation, martyrs avoid where masochists—and fools—rush in, or at least do not
flee. In this 'foolish' stance, the 'normal' instinct to flee itself takes
flight, and it is impossible to tell if, in a masochistic moment, one is
well-rooted or just plain stubborn.

In his unheroic stance, stuck fast, the masochist is compelled to
bow before the gods. Trapped in the painful knowledge of his own
inadequacies, he suffers the internal, often invisible, humiliation of
his humanity. The masochist is close to an almost religious, usually
unconscious conviction that he has nothing to lose. He hovers,
trembling, at the edge of Simone Weil's insight that one can always

be deprived by circumstances of what one is proud. Therefore pride is a lie, and humility consists in the apprehension of this lie. If he is not seduced into autoerotic tailspins or into the gleaming armor of the martyr, a masochist might reach a real humility.

To realize that pride is a lie brings one close to a paradisiacal moment and also expulsion from paradise, because it is a moment of ineffable closeness to God and immeasurable distance from him. Adam and Eve were close to God not just because they fell first, but because they fell at all. Trying to reach or preserve that closeness, masochists fall and fall, then fall again. Barred from the Garden, they reach for heaven by plunging to hell. For them, there is a beatitude in the beating.

Martyrdom and masochism embody different attitudes toward suffering. Suffering, from the martyr's perspective, is something to avoid, something to manipulate for the ego's use (and abuse). The masochist moves in a wider sphere. He does not ask "Why me," but rather, "How" and "What for." By standing under it, he might understand the suffering—its nature and purpose. Masochism functions to relativize and radicalize the ego. As such, it is a deeper, dirtier experience.

Admittedly, these images of the martyr and the masochist are too extreme and idealized for actual life. These two modes or attitudes are constantly shifting and changing, and both are present to one degree or another in any individual. The pathology of martyrdom, its soul-killing through projection and ego-identification, might be a door through which one can enter into psychological masochism, and thus move into the deeper mysteries and paradoxes of soul.

A Deflection:
Prometheus: A Mythological Case Study

'Masochist' and 'martyr' are more like masks worn in a play than categorical labels. One takes them on and puts them off. "Now you see it, now you don't." Keeping these masks with us to lend both cover and differentiation for these two roles, we attend the masque by Aeschylus, *Prometheus Bound*.

Enter the Titan Prometheus, friend and champion of the human race, a savior who teaches humans the arts and crafts of civilization to ensure their survival against the gods' hostility and power.

Some legends say it was Prometheus who actually created humans, forming them from clay and infusing them with life from fire. But it is as savior-thief that Prometheus is best known. He steals fire from the Olympian gods to give to humankind, a gift of consciousness, power, light in the darkness. Prometheus's name probably comes from the Greek word meaning "foresight" or "forethought." He gives that fire of divine consciousness, or forethought, that distinguishes the human race. By his actions and by his very nature, Prometheus is a prototype or image of humankind. It is his necessity to engage in a titanic struggle with his fate.

By stealing the gods' fire, Prometheus transfers some of their power, some of their divinity, to humans, so that they become "like God." Thus he transgresses the will of Zeus, father of the Olympians. This fiery knowledge must be stolen, just as Eve snatched it from God's tree in Eden, and once stolen it cannot be returned. The theft is not reversible; it is only punishable.

In his great sin, Prometheus, as portrayed by Aeschylus, is a study in resistance and submission. The play is full of exclamations that Prometheus will never repent, never give in to the will of Zeus. By his nature as a Titan (from a Greek word meaning "to overreach

oneself''), which is dark, unconscious, lacking fire, Prometheus, like
a human being, is compelled to his crime to seek the light. It is his
mythic role, his fate, to steal the fire. And it is his fate, as well, to be
punished. The 'must' of Prometheus's act is determined by Necessity. Prometheus says, "for I know well against necessity, / against
its strength, no one can fight and win" (Ll. 105–06).

Prometheus knows his sin, his punishment, and his necessity. Of
the fire theft, he proclaims,

> This is the sin committed
> for which I stand accountant, and I pay
> nailed in my chains under the open sky.
>
> (Ll. 112–14)

> I knew,
> I knew when I transgressed nor will deny it.
>
> (Ll. 267–68)

Prometheus has done what is necessary, has followed his fate, but he
has done it with an excess of pride. He suffers unjustly in his own
view. It is an ancient dilemma and a common question: why should
we be punished for doing what is necessary and in accordance with
our own natures?

Prometheus rails against the insult of his punishment, stands on
his Promethean dignity, sets himself to resist, and calls upon
everyone to bemoan the terrible injustice of Zeus's decree. "Look at
me, then, in chains. . . ." This eternal human predicament portrays
an essential and noble spirit of humankind: proud, fighting, railing,
enduring. In his nobility and dignity, Prometheus is more hero than
martyr or masochist.

Prometheus's punishment is horror-filled. He is chained and
nailed on a lonely mountain crag. Day after day an eagle tears at his
liver, which grows whole again at night. There is no real reprieve in

the coming of night, for this only precedes and makes possible the agony of the next day. We may see in this the timeless suffering of human nobility and pride—and in Titanic doses, the suffering of a pathology.

Impaled on the conviction of the complete justice of his cause, Prometheus does not lessen in his resistance. Zeus eventually offers to release him if he will reveal his secret foreknowledge concerning which of Zeus's sons will overthrow Zeus. This is a most fascinating and ironic offer. The same forethought which was once used against Zeus in the fire-theft is now asked in return as the price of freedom. In effect, Prometheus can gain his freedom if he will sacrifice or submit something of his very essence to his tormentor. This is the crucial moment of the drama, the moment of truth—not because it offers a way out for Prometheus, but because it presses upon him the fateful reality that there is no way out. There can be no fair bargain struck, no smile-and-handshake peace treaty, between Prometheus and Zeus. Full liberation requires full submission. And the full submission required is not just *to* Zeus but *of* Prometheus, not just something Prometheus *has* but something Prometheus *is*. Yet, in an all-too-familiar counter-move, Prometheus refuses to tell the secret *until* Zeus releases him. So they remain locked in motionless battle, a cold war of wills. No more concessions till the other side disarms, no disarmament until the other side concedes.

Some of our themes in masochism and martyrdom begin to coincide in this contest of wills between Prometheus and Zeus. Martyr, masochist, and Prometheus all resist, and all suffer, in their own different ways behind distinctive masks. The martyr, who endured some rough treatment in this chapter, avoids psychological movement by staying victim. He uses his victim position to victimize others, rising above his suffering in an inflated balloon of moral superiority. The masochist suffers more than his share of humiliation and pain, even though he often manufactures off-the-point transgressions. He submits and suffers—passionately, compulsively. He cannot do otherwise.

Prometheus and the masochist are bound together, back-to-back, by reverse compulsions: the masochist *must submit* to everyone, everything; Prometheus *cannot submit* to anyone, anything. Unlike the martyr, Prometheus *does* suffer, *must* suffer, enduring the horrible regularity of his punishment. But like the martyr, he is certain that his punishment is unjust. In this certainty, he misses the real point of his punishment, that the issue does not center around justice at all, but the manner in which he suffers the penalty.

Prometheus was proud of his craftiness and strength, proud he stole the fire, proud he could be punished without submitting, proud he could withhold his liberating secret. A masochist has a parallel pride: no one can outdo him in the art and extremity of subjection. No one submits better, sooner; no one bends to deeper degradation with more finesse, style, and endurance.

Masochism is an art of holding oneself in oppositional extremity. The masochist sees himself living—appears to live—*in extremis*, at the very edge of danger, madness, death. A masochist's pleasure is extremely painful and his pain, extremely pleasurable. Often opposite feelings like pride and humiliation are present simultaneously, both torturous, both pleasurable. In the midst of such emotional extremity, the need and feeding of the masochistic compulsion is clearly, itself, part of the torture and pleasure. There is a pride in this cliff-hanging extremity, in maintaining these impossible oppositions without plunging over the edge. It is an extreme pride, a pride of extremity, of going to extremes and surviving. It is a pride of promethean proportions.

In his pride, Prometheus both hides behind, and reveals himself through, the masks of martyrdom and masochism. Oceanos tells Prometheus,

> Know yourself and reform your ways to new ways. . . .
> you are not yet humble, still you do not yield
> to your misfortunes. . . .
>
> (Ll. 310 ff)

The Greek injunction to "know yourself," when applied to humans, meant "know that you are human and nothing more." Prometheus does not know his own limitations, nor that he must be bound to see them. Indeed, from his perspective, being Prometheus and having limitations are mutually exclusive. In this stance, he shows the face of the martyr. Perhaps Prometheus's most important transgression is that he does not recognize *what* he must yield to. In his eyes, Zeus is the oppressor. But Oceanos tells him that it is not Prometheus's torturer, but his *misfortunes* which must be yielded to. Prometheus must escape the martyr fantasy and move into a posture of *amor fati*—that love of fate which is one characteristic of authentic masochism. The call here is to submit to his natural inadequacies, to the shame attached to them, and especially to the inevitable consequences of his own spirit.

The purpose of Prometheus's punishment is that ". . . he may learn to endure and like / the sovereignty of Zeus. . ." (Ll. 10 f). There is a masochistic tinge to this pronouncement. The way out of this impossibly polarized situation—proud, unyielding, rebel Prometheus vs. proud, unyielding, Establishment Zeus—requires Prometheus to learn not only to "endure" the sovereignty of Zeus, but to "like" it. Prometheus needs a touch of masochism to release him from bondage; he needs to enjoy his submission and subjection.

Either polarity—extreme promethean pride or extreme promethean humiliation—is still only a partial vision. In his inability to do anything but submit, the masochist refuses all power, all 'rightness.' He appears as *only* wrong, lowly, totally dispossessed of worth. He sees his lowliness and sin as personal, and thus as personally punishable—and he usually is blind to the personal pride in this attitude. At a masochistic extreme, he does not truly submit, but grovels instead. This groveling, like its counterpole of unbending pride, only leaves one isolated in chains, nailed on a lonely mountain peak.

The daughters of Oceanos, impressed by Prometheus's wonderful inventions and care for mankind, hope that one day, freed, he will be as strong as Zeus. But Prometheus replies that Fate's appointed end has not yet been realized: "I must be bowed by age-long pain and grief." This statement has a cadence as relentless as Fate itself. Slowly Prometheus begins to realize that his sufferings come less from an overt crime than from his inability to submit to suffering and limitation. Slowly, he begins to understand that his promethean spirit has become its own punishment. He sees that accusations of blame and injustice, heroically shouted from the mountain top, have blinded him to the deeper purpose of Fate working within his bondage. "I must be bowed." To accept this is to be humbled; and to be humbled is to be freed.

*

In the introduction we spoke of mythology as a mouthing of soul.[2] The mythological words and sounds of Prometheus carry telling messages which connect us with our fate. Like Prometheus, we are bound to our fate, accompanied by gods who make our way as well as stand in it. But our experience is thankless, shallow, and lacking in meaning without a recognition of Fate. Prometheus always stands close behind us, his mighty and foolish hand on our shoulders, his impassioned cries echoing through us as we learn to hear, speak—and even love—our fates.

CHAPTER 6

Dionysus, or The Madness of Masochism

> *Pentheus: Do you hold your rites during*
> *the day or night?*
> *Dionysus: Mostly by night. The darkness*
> *is well suited to devotion.*
> EURIPIDES, *The Bacchae*

> *I say I'll go through fire*
> *And I'll go through fire*
> *As he wants it, so it will be.*
> *Crazy he calls me, sure I'm crazy,*
> *Crazy in love, you see.*
> *Like the wind that shakes the bough*
> *He moves me with a smile....*
> *Crazy he calls me, sure I'm crazy....*
> BILLIE HOLIDAY, "Crazy He Calls Me"

*

Thus I lie,
Writhing, twisting, tormented
With all eternal tortures,
Hit
By thee, cruelest hunter,
Thou unknown *god*!

Hit deeper!
Hit once more yet!
Drive a stake through and break this heart!
Why this torture

...

Only torture, torture?
Why torture *me*,
Delighted by suffering, thou unknown god?

. . .

What wouldst thou gain by torture,
Thou torturer!
Thou hangman-god!
Or should I, doglike,
Roll before thee?

. . .

What wilt thou, unknown—god?

What? Ransom?
Why wilt thou ransom?
Demand much! Thus my pride advises.
And make thy speech short! That my other
    pride advises.

Hah, hah!
Me thou wilt have? Me?
Me—entirely?

. . .

Away!
He himself fled,
My last, only companion,
My great enemy,
My unknown,
My hangman-god.

No! Do come back
With all thy tortures!
To the last of all that are lonely,
Oh, come back!
All my tear-streams run
Their course to thee;
And my heart's final flame—
Flares up for *thee*!

Oh, come back,
My unknown god! My *pain*! My last
—happiness!
Nietzsche, *Thus Spake Zarathustra*

This wrenching passage from Nietzsche takes us to the heart of—what shall we call it?—religious masochism? Religious madness? The madness of masochistic religion? The dominant/submissive complex? Christian mysticism? The Dionysian experience? Each adds something, but no one term is sufficient.

In Dionysus, the threads we have been spinning out thus far—humiliation and submission, pleasure and ecstasy, suffering and madness, death and mortification, sexuality and religiosity, necessity and fate—come together to tie a knot of paradox. The realm of Dionysus is best described by the god's epithets. He is "The Dark One," "The Joyful One," "The Dancer and Ecstatic Lover," "The Giver of Riches," "The Delight of Mortals," "The Deliverer," and "The Liberator." He is known as "The Mad One," "The Raging One," "The Frenzied One," "The Nocturnal One," "The Subterranean," and "He Who Wanders in the Night." He is "The Erect," "The Betesticled," "The Man Without True Virility," "The Womanly One," and "The Womanly Stranger." The realm of Dionysus is a realm of paradox; he is "The Hybrid," "The God of Two Forms" and "The God of Many Forms," and finally, "The Lord of Souls."

Looking through the many forms of masochism—the madness in ecstasy and the pleasure in submission and mortification—we see the Lord of Souls in a divine epiphany. His coming is a visitation, and to turn away invites a madness without ecstasy. A style of consciousness—a Dionysian consciousness—which allows for masochistic experience can see "visitation" as a welcome opportunity rather than as a pathology. ''Visitation,'' wrote novelist Charles Morgan, ''is necessary, and whoever has been made aware of the possibility of it waits for it always; his life has no other continuous meaning or purpose.''[1] In those moments when the Lord of Souls visits the soul with a madness that we call masochism, we may see masochism as *an act and experience of worship.*

The aim of the cult of Dionysus was ecstasis, which ''could mean anything from 'taking you out of yourself' to a profound alteration of personality.''[2] The masochistic experience, whether expressed sexually or not, has a similar aim. Karen Horney hypothesized that

> all masochistic strivings are ultimately directed toward satisfaction, namely, toward the goal of oblivion, of getting rid of self with all its conflicts and all its limitations. The masochistic phenomena which we find in neuroses would then represent a pathological modification of the dionysian tendencies which seem to be spread throughout the world.[3]

Horney was probably right about the goal of oblivion in masochism. Certainly the ecstasy of oblivion is a feature of Dionysian as well as masochistic experience, where the individual is so taken out of himself that his individual identity is extinguished. But psychiatry has consistently equated this desire for oblivion with pathology. In former times, in a less secular age, it was regarded as a striving for union with the Godhead, and its ecstasy was mystical. How do we distinguish between pathology and worship? Or between gross exhibitionism and dramatic ecstasy? Consider the case of Elizabeth of Genton, a medieval nun whose brief story is recounted by Krafft-Ebing as an instance of pathological masochism:

> As a result of whipping she actually passed into a state of bacchanalian madness. As a rule, she raved when, excited by unusual flagellation, she believed herself united with her ''ideal.'' This condition was so exquisitely

pleasant to her that she would frequently cry out, "O love, O eternal love, O love, O you creatures! cry out with me: 'Love, Love!' "⁴

If we look for pathology, no doubt we will find it—in the excess, the whipping, the bacchanalian madness, the love. We will likewise find it in all the saints. "In nearly every saint's life we find attempts to draw nearer to the suffering Christ through self-inflicted pains."⁵ It would appear that Christian sainthood requires a healthy dose of masochism. But then, we usually regard saints as a bit mad.

At Pompeii there is a series of ancient frescoes in the Villa of Mysteries believed to depict a woman's initiation into the mysteries of Dionysus. It is impossible to reproduce the silent, haunting beauty of these paintings, let alone in word-pictures. But these illustrations, and two or three in particular, illuminate our theme in mythic enactment. We can read this initiation scene as an initiation of soul, through submission, to *enthusiasmos*—possession by the god.

In one scene occurring near the end of the series, the woman initiate, semi-nude in a loose-falling robe, kneels beside a clothed, seated woman, her head resting in the seated figure's lap. Behind her stands an angel-like feminine figure, winged, feet placed wide apart, her right arm holding an upraised whip. There is a calmness, almost a melancholy silence, about this scene. It is impossible to know whether the first blow is just about to fall or whether the whipping is already underway. This scene conveys a sense of anticipation and imminence—not unlike countless masochistic fantasies involving whipping and punishment. The suggestive nakedness of the woman, her kneeling posture, her total lack of resistance to the poised whip compose a supreme visual image of complete submission. She is prepared to receive the god. How did she come to be in this position?

The scene immediately preceding the whipping shows the woman kneeling, trying to lift the cover from a basket which contains the phallus, and thus the god. This effort is usually interpreted as presumptuous, even sacrilegious.

Art historian Amadeo Maiui has suggested that the winged figure with the whip personifies our now familiar goddess *Aidos*,[6] whose name means "Shame" (awe, reverence, respect, modesty). The initiate is then scourged by shame, or modesty, to humble her, to restore a proper perspective of her natural limitations, her humanity and mortality.

> She has brought this [Dionysian] vision back to the daylight, but she is distraught from its influence, and has lost her humanity and feeling. She is presumptuous in wanting to unveil the sacred symbol of the god, and inaccessible to the counsel of others—that is, the women standing behind her—but here, the feeling of modesty [Aidos] which she has lost in the face of the Holy One, approaches her as a rescuing and avenging angel.[7]

From the Greek meaning of the word "angel," we can see that the winged figure is a "messenger." Like the Christian evangels, she brings a redemptive message. The whip is the medium of her message, and like the medium, the message has to do with the suffering of shame and the shame of suffering.

The initiate's complete submission makes possible the *ecstasis* that follows in the next scene. Here, a nude woman begins an elegant, graceful dance, clapping small cymbals over her head while behind her a light veil billows out, as if lifted by the breath of the god. It is a dance of complete liberation, an experience which can only follow total submission to the god.

As in the rites of Dionysus, punishment and correction are important and common experiences for most of us, and take on even greater importance when there is a tendency in us to interpret both chance events and natural consequences as personal messages, affirming or condemning our actions and feelings. This tendency carries an important psychological truth. After all, punishments and corrections are to educate us. And as we are taught the ways of the world, as we experience the necessity for change and, indeed, for grace, we often feel less initiated and purified than punished and corrected.

For the masochist, punishment may be the central theme of his life. In modern pornography, when the naked woman is kneeling under the whip, there is usually an assumed crime for which she is being disciplined. In everyday life as well, the masochist's basis of relationship to the people and things in his world is that they are the punishers, he is the punished. In the most predictable and common events, from bad weather to stubbed toes, he finds proofs of his unworthiness. In his secret pride, a masochist may stay only personal, blithely unaware that original sin does not originate with him. Pondering, suffering, reliving his routine humiliations and pains, the masochist takes the center—even if that center is a whipping post.

In their fantasies, masochists create all manner of rules to be broken so that they may themselves be punished. Whether these fantasies are acted out, held inside, or fitted to life events afterward to explain or justify, they provide the masochist with constant rediscovery and re-experience of his inferiority and disobedience. But this chronic activity of rule-making/breaking and punishment is ambiguous and ambivalent: for, while the masochist feels he deserves punishment, what he gets is always too extreme. It is always cruel and inhuman; if punishments were less so, the punisher would not be called a sadist. If he talks back, the masochist must crawl across the room on his belly; if he is late, he gets thirty lashes; if he shows the slightest sexual awareness, he is raped.

But the masochist, often unconsciously, experiences a deeper justice by means of his fantasies. The apparent 'crime' conceals a deeper crime, one for which he must grope in the dark. This deeper crime, shadily obscured by its extreme opposite of humiliation, is pride, that most original of human sins.

As with the Dionysian initiate, this deeper crime consists of a wrong attitude: pride in the form of inflation, presumption, arrogance. A masochist may reveal this attitude in many ways. He may feel himself the best of the worst, the most consummate sufferer in the deepest pain. He may feel like the most deserving who gets the least reward, the most incompetent person with the highest potential, the mortal most singled out for harassment from Fate. The best worm in the universe, the masochist might feel he deserves *no* punishment, *less* punishment, or the *best* punishment—or all three at once. Whether in confession, delirium, analysis, fantasy, or wine-loosened tongue, one's truth will out.

Masochists tend to walk a thin line, knowing, then losing, then knowing that sense of difference between punishment and purification. "Handle with holy care the violent wand of god!"[8] The whip in the Pompeii scene is probably a *thyrsus*, a sacred branch used in Dionysus's cult. The god is present in the thyrsus, which is the vehicle of dangerous, natural forces. Its use in cult, according to the classical scholar E. R. Dodds, is an act of "controlled violence," an attempt to subdue these natural forces to a religious purpose. "The thyrsus is the vehicle of these forces; its touch can work beneficent miracles, but it can also inflict injury, and . . . can cause madness."[9]

Use of a profane object profanes the ritual, hence the god; and this profanes and debases the worshipper, whose motive and emotion are no longer religious. One can't help thinking of the prevalence of caning, "the English vice," used for punishment and sexual stimulation. To use the rod *solely* in irreligious attitudes, from the viewpoint of Dionysian religion, is a profanation. The god is not present in the object; rather, the object itself has become a god in the form of a fetish.

There is high value given and close attention paid to the instrument of pain in countless masochistic fantasies. Like the holy *thyrsus*, the instrument is the symbol, the scepter of divinity. While many fantasies include other forms of torture, such as humiliating postures or words or sexual stimulation itself, many more center around—or at least include—instruments of torture. The possibilities for instruments are limitless, and many fantasies are strikingly meticulous. There are willow whips, bullwhips, knotted whips, weighted whips, metal whips, and cat-o'-nine-tails; there are canes, sticks, and boards of every length, width, shape, and thickness, and from every kind of tree; there is every imaginable style of belt, with and without buckles and studs; there are hairbrushes, pliers, toothpicks, spatulas, needles, electric cords, cattle prods, spurs, knives, jewelry, chastity belts, and scissors. The list goes on and on, fulsome and awful as one's imagination. In masochistic fantasy, the instrument is usually replete with distinctive detail, numinous with a beauty and ugliness and fear which create and preserve just the right sensations.

This ritualization seems to have as its purpose the restoration of some religious meaning through ritual objects. Even in the barest and most common beating fantasies, we can hear the sharp hymn of the holy thyrsus as it slices down on the supplicant's back. There is the feeling and the rhythm of a beating too in the throbbing compulsiveness of masochism. One cannot escape the beating, the ritual, the fantasy. Its extremity and need bear testimony through *re-petition*, which means both "to attack again" and "to ask again," or here particularly, "to ask *for* it again."

As "to suffer" means "to bear below," "to submit," or "to undergo," "to relate" means "to bear back," "to return," "to carry something again." One returns inevitably, necessarily, as to a memorial or monument, to one's places of trauma and fate, to the things that must be learned and remembered. Suffering and relationship go together. As one analysand discovered, "a beating can have the rhythm of lovemaking."

"Relate" also means "to tell again," to repeat the same theme, the same fantasy, the same shame, the same desire. Repetition and relationship—interpersonal or intrapsychic—go together.

> Repetition and returning are integral aspects of the cyclical phenomenology of relationship; that is, always returning to the same place, the same argument, the same words, the same feelings, the same mistakes. People complain of following the same pattern over and over again. This repeating, this "again-ness" of relationship is unavoidable—one of its necessary qualities.[10]

The soul and its fantasies seek refinement through repetition. By experiencing religion in ritual, and refinement in repetition, a masochist may begin to move from the compulsion of blind necessity to the deeper meanings of fate.

*

To see masochism from within the realm of Dionysus is to see behind it the shape of Dionysian madness. In this place of myth and religion, we see less a disease than a divine epiphany. Madness partakes in delight and horror, truth in illusion, and delusion in truth. Dionysus is the "Master of Magical Illusions." The god Dionysus is full of paradox, and to see from his perspective is to see the world both as it is and is not, to see both sides as equally true, equally illusory. In the God of Wine there is truth—*in vino veritas*—and there is illusion, just as there is profound truth and magical illusion in the disjointed speech and hallucinatory visions of madmen. In one sense, the Mad God is a mirror, reflecting our own true madness. Masoch requires a mirror in his novel to reflect the truth and illusion of the madness in masochism: the presumption and modesty, the substantial reality and ephemeral appearances. The fixed, motionless "smiling mask" Dionysus wears is an illusion, but it mirrors a truth. The realm of Dionysus is a realm where truth and illusion happen together, and it is madness to separate them.

Masochism, its paradoxical nature intact, moves us from the conceptual realm to the imaginal, from superficial appearances (masochistic sex, deviant behavior) to the dark depths of passion and suffering.

The dark side, which all of the forms of Dionysus suddenly turn toward us, demonstrates that they do not originate in the superficial play of existence but in its depths. Dionysus himself, who raises life into the heights of ecstasy, is the suffering god. The raptures which he brings rise from the innermost stirrings of that which lives. But wherever these depths are agitated, there, along with rapture and birth, rise up also horror and ruin.[11]

Scholars are divided as to how literal one central feature of the Dionysian cult was: the rending and tearing and eating of raw flesh. To those who experience it, it is "a mixture of supreme exaltation and supreme repulsion; it is at once holy and horrible, fulfillment and uncleanness, a sacrament and a pollution. . . ."[12] Dionysian experience rises up from a depth of the soul which is pre-literate, before the Word, alien to all rationality. Dionysus himself

is the monstrous creature which lives in the depths. From its mask it looks out at man and sends him reeling with the ambiguity of nearness and remoteness, of life and death in one. Its divine intelligence holds the contradictions together. For it is the spirit of excitation and wildness, and everything alive, which seethes and glows, resolves the schism between itself and its opposite and has already absorbed this spirit in its desire. Thus all earthly powers are united in the god: the generating, nourishing, intoxicating rapture; the life-giving inexhaustibility; and the tearing pain, the deathly pallor, the speechless night of having been. He is the mad ecstasy which hovers over every conception and birth and whose wildness is always ready to move on to destruction and death. He is life which, when it overflows, grows mad and in its profoundest passion is intimately associated with death.[13]

Dionysus, persecuted and dismembered in his youth, calls the soul to vulnerability, woundedness, dismemberment, the torture of not being re-membered. He irresistibly pulls the soul downward to a dark depth where there is no light of conscious life. One of my patients, giving me a written masochistic fantasy after long internal struggle and resistance, said in blushing and rushing words: "Here it is. This is what I came to therapy for. It's terrible. It's sick. It's wonderful, I hate it, it's my favorite fantasy. I can't stand it, I love it. It's disgusting. I don't want to stop it."

This tumble of contradictory responses reveals an understandably conflicted attitude towards submission, suffering, pleasure, worship, and indeed, towards death itself. The conscious personality passionately resists precisely that experience for which the soul most violently yearns. In the worship, in the submission, there is an inevitable surrender and submergence of the ego. This is not the suicide of hopeless depression, nor the unconscious mania of the accident-prone, nor the conscious self-termination of the ill and/or aged. It is, rather, the soul's intolerable longing for liberation, the wild rush into death as one rushes madly into the arms of a lover.

Masochism acquires its full meaning and significance only when related to death,

> imagined as an ecstatic release, as something the soul wants and needs and which it receives through the discovery of an intense, overwhelming value of the flesh and its exquisite enjoyment, which is also our worst pain. Suppose masochism as a death experience and quite bothersome for life. Suppose, at the same time, that masochism makes possible a union of soul and flesh, impossible so intensely in any other way.[14]

"We run to death," sings the Chorus in *The Bacchae*. It is death as ultimate union, death as the soul's truest home (the Underworld), death as the realm of psyche unencumbered by body and literalization. Sometimes love and death are so alike as to become the measure of each other; lovers like Romeo and Juliet die to each other, for each other, and without each other. No wonder the French call orgasm *la petite morte*. What love and death have in common is extinction of personal ego, the terrifying loss of self-definition, decisiveness, action, and also liberation from these same burdens. While the natural, directive thrust of ego is upward and on-ward, ever extending its sphere of influence, masochistic submission moves downwards with the gradient into cool death, obedient to the force of gravity.

In his later work, Freud called the drive for death Thanatos, after the Greek god of Death, and placed it on equal ground with Eros, the drive for Love, or desire for Pleasure. Love and Death, Relatedness and Oblivion are the two basic drives in life, the strongest extremes. They are the mainstays of masochistic ex-perience. Before Dionysus, the tragic, mad god of suffering and joy, the Maenads flung themselves in rapturous destruction. They were thereby not only degraded, but also initiated, exalted, and redeemed.

*

Wanda says to Severin, in Masoch's *Venus in Furs*:

> I can indeed imagine belonging to one man for life, but he would have to be a real man who commands my respect and enslaves me by his innate power.... And I know from experience that as soon as a man falls in love he becomes weak, pliable and ridiculous; he surrenders to the woman and goes down on his knees to her. And I could only love a man before whom I myself should have to kneel.[15]

Dionysus, as the "god of women," is a way into archetypally feminine experience; as the bisexual god, "The Man-Womanish," he is also a way out of genderized masochism.

Psychiatry has generally thought of masochism as a biological characteristic given with genes, a characteristic of gender. To Freud and Krafft-Ebing, this was an assumption needing no proof:

> In women, voluntary subjection to the opposite sex is a physiological phenomenon. Owing to her passive role in procreation and long-existent social conditions, ideas of subjection are, in woman, normally connected

with the idea of sexual relations. They form, so to speak, the harmonics which determine the tone-quality of feminine feeling. . . . An attentive observer of life may still easily recognize how the custom of unnumbered generations, in connection with the passive role with which woman has been endowed by Nature, has given her an instinctive inclination to voluntary subordination to man; he will notice that exaggeration of customary gallantry is very distasteful to women, and that a deviation from it in the direction of masterful behavior, though loudly reprehended, is often accepted with secret satisfaction. Under the veneer of polite society the instinct of feminine servitude is everywhere discernible.[16]

Masochism is influenced, but not bound, by the presence or absence of sex organs and hormones. Its essence of paradox, of pleasure/pain, necessarily pushes its roots deep into the imaginal. We experience masochism in close connection with the experiences of our bodies. But their literal gender is not the essence of the experience. If masochism were explainable according to physiological gender, it might be easier to agree with Krafft-Ebing that some degree of masochism is "normal" in women but "abnormal" in men. If we identified with our literal genders, we then would tend to moralize while we demoralized the soul.

The real question is not whether masochism is "feminine," but whether "feminine" is synonymous with "woman" or "female." To speak of "masculine" and "feminine" is not to speak of men and women, but of metaphorical, qualitative attitudes. These qualities of primal femininity belong to both men and women; they are psychological, not biological, qualities.

In our confusion of language—not knowing how to talk about psyche or how to talk psychologically—we have assumed too often that 'dominant' is synonymous with 'superior.' When Feminists protest male domination, they are—just as importantly—protesting the supposed superiority of the masculine which this domination assumes. On the other side, people have equated feminine 'submission' with female 'inferiority,' deriving all sorts of dogmas about the 'natural order' from the equation. Other insidious equations have arisen, included in much psychoanalytic theory, all of which indicate that little differentiation has been made between psychic fantasy and literal doings.

A submissive individual in a sexual encounter is not necessarily passive, inferior, or a victim in the rest of his—or her—life. After all, 'S-M' partners sometimes switch roles. One partner accepts this submissive role, not because of genes, but in response to a dual fantasy between himself and his partner. His submissiveness is a psychic fantasy—as much his partner's fantasy as his—acted out in flesh and blood. It is the submissiveness that is the important quality—not the gender of the figure who embodies it. So it is incorrect to speak of "feminine masochism" if "feminine" is meant to apply to women alone, for masochism is a fantasy common to both males and females. It is correct to speak of masochism as "feminine," in that it is a fantasy of submission. In terms of qualities and values, we may certainly call masochism, as Freud did, an expression of feminine (not female) nature: its passivity, relatedness, eroticism, inertia, etc.

Masochism is one of the soul's ways of restoring value to what has been devalued. Its persistence through time, its compulsive and pleasure-yielding nature, its demand for and love of the aesthetic in sexuality, its search for religious essence, its inherent sense of pathology and deviance—indeed, its extremity in all these aspects—all bear witness to its value. Yet today, the devaluation of masochistic qualities is so severe that psychiatry actually considers an addiction to suffering more perverse than an addiction to legally prescribed drugs intended to relieve suffering. In our age, which regards nearly all suffering as a disease or a moral failure, masochism is a statement of the soul's need and desire for suffering.

The strength and power of Dionysus appear, to a heroic consciousness, as weakness, submissiveness, and passivity. Dionysus appears as victim. He allows his mortal cousin Pentheus to manacle and humiliate him; he promises complete feminine surrender as the price of bringing his mother Semele back from the Underworld; he is often frightened and defeated in the face of tough masculinity.

We might speak of a "Dionysian femininity," or an expression and consciousness of a primal femininity which is Dionysian in nature—dark, obscure, silently melancholy and ambiguous, joyful and suffering. Dionysus's victories come in liquid form, from wine, from indirect subtle stirrings, and from a clever and almost perverse manipulation of his enemies. Nor does he win his followers by force. He wines and dines them, possessing them as he nourishes them. "The Womanly One" seduces, lures, smiles enigmatically to entice his devotees, drawing them in a wily, artful dance to the deepest recesses of feminine, man-less wilderness—the forest, the mountains, the night.

Yet Dionysus appears as victim. For most of us, "victimization" appears inflicted upon us (by victors, robbers, rapists) when we lack strength to resist. Here "victim" means to be powerless and/or at a disadvantage against an oppressor. But in Dionysus we see "victim" as a state of being occurring in nature, a condition of the feminine soul of readiness to sacrifice (Latin *victima* meaning "sacrifice"). Dionysus releases his followers from victimization and oppression by calling them to be sacrifices. He sanctifies victimhood. Those who reject and scorn him do not recognize, to their peril, that there is a hidden divinity in this victim. Refusal to acknowledge the strange, bisexual ambiguity of this god results in insanity and death. In Jung's phrase, the god becomes a disease.

Masochism disallows the devaluation of both archetypal femininity and madness. To Western thinking, femininity has been viewed as a disease, and all its qualities—e.g., passivity, ambiguity, emotionality—as symptoms. Madness has been perfunctorily dismissed as 'unreal,' a pack of lies. This negatively masculine context adds still more fuel to the experience of elemental femininity as a kind of Dionysian madness.

> This archetypal world of the feminine knows nothing of the laws and regulations which govern human society, and no breath of the spirit which streams forth from the goddess of marriage, Hera, has touched it. It is a world which conforms completely to nature. To burst the bonds of marital duty and domestic custom in order to follow the torch of the god over the mountain tops and fill the forests with wild shrieks of exultation—this is the purpose for which Dionysus stirs up the women.[17]

"To burst the bonds" is the purpose of both Dionysian and masochistic experience. Both break out of a style of consciousness which has become a bondage. It is indeed strange that this is done through another form of bondage, through servitude to this madness which is the god himself. Yet the stronger the bonds of law, duty, and custom, the more urgent the claim of Dionysus in the opposite direction.

Strength can be a terrible burden. It is a bondage which must be relieved in moments of abandonment, of weakness, of letting down and letting go. So it is hardly surprising that the strong personality—male or female—should be the most likely to desire masochistic experiences. Nancy Friday relates one woman's favorite fantasy of being tied to the bed by her lover, who then stares at her nakedness which humiliates her deliciously; when she begs to be released, he finally enters her. As interesting as her fantasy are her comments:

> It seems that the more liberated I become (I'm really digging Women's Lib now) the more I fantasize about the spanking and the bondage. Since I'm fully liberated in my work situation, social life, etc., it's almost as if I'm trying to achieve some sort of counter-balance to this liberation in my sexual life. . . . I am sure there are other women like me, who having emerged from being under male domination, crave to return to it in bed.[18]

That which is unknown and 'other' exerts a strong pull. It is not surprising that one should seek dominance in the opposite sex, precisely because it is opposite. As the Other, the Unknown, the opposite cannot be readily identified with; thus to experience it, one must reach a place of submission to it. Its otherness, because it flexes and refreshes the personality, produces an even more complete and satisfying submission. The masochistic experience, sexually expressed, is at the same time a religious experience, a supplication and submission to the Other who has taken on the quality of a divinity. In *L'Aveu (Confession)*, we find Adamov's expression of the craving for just such an experience:

> I want to be humbled by woman, and by woman alone, because she is "the other" *par excellence*, the outsider, the opposite of myself. Woman is the image of everything which rises up from the depths and possesses the lure of the abyss. The lower one sinks, the lower one wants to sink. Having fallen to the bottom of the world, I seek an even deeper nether world in the thrall of woman. I want to be lower than the lowest.[19]

Woman here is the goddess of the Netherworld. Submission to an inferior being is degrading, but submission to a god or goddess is a measure of the soul's true worth. Dionysus may appear in either a male or female body, and when he does, he calls to something dark and inscrutable and overwhelming in the soul, driving it into an orgy of passionate sexual abandonment and calm submission.

It is said that when Aphrodite (Love) emerged from the sea, Aidos was one of those attendant upon her. There is a root connection between Love and Shame, particularly sensual love and shame as modesty or reticence. Aidos is a daughter of Night, and so guards with her dark wings the secrets that belong to the night.[20] Her presence in this initiation to the rites of Dionysus insures that the religious meaning and the fundamental sexuality of the experience are kept together. Aidos embodies not only the sense of religious shame (humility, reverence), but also the under- and over-tone of sexual excitement, the shame of exposure, of being revealed in body and soul to one's Lover, as well as to one's God. By throwing her black wings over the secrets of night, Aidos maintains that secrecy and privacy of sex which mark it as sacramental.

In masochistic experience, every bit of flesh comes alive in an agony of trembling ecstasy. All is sensitized almost beyond endurance. How can it *not* be sexual? How can it *not* be religious? One is taken out of oneself and beyond all law and duty and custom, and yet utterly reduced, pressed down, made small. It is a defeat and a glory.

*

> The madness which is called Dionysus is no sickness, no debility in life, but a companion of life at its healthiest. It is the tumult which erupts from its innermost recesses when they mature and force their way to the surface. It is the madness inherent in the womb of the mother. This attends all moments of creation, constantly changes ordered existence into chaos, and ushers in primal salvation and primal pain—and in both, the primal wildness of being.[21]

Once this impulsive life-force has broken loose, the whole world feels its irresistible effect. Nature is no longer divided into animal and divine. "'O Bromius!' they cried until the beasts and all the mountain seemed wild with divinity. And when they ran, everything ran with them."[22]

"The Dionysian," says Jung, "is the horror of the annihilation of the *principium individuationis* and at the same time 'rapturous delight' in its destruction. It is therefore comparable to intoxication, which dissolves the individual into his collective instincts and components—an explosion of the isolated ego through the world."[23]

Although we cannot make specific gender identifications in our attempts to define masochism, we can still see sex itself as a basic vehicle of masochistic expression. Whether sexuality is covert and implicit, a faintly sensed far-off rhythm, or overt and explicit, hot-blooded and pulsing, it flows through all masochistic phenomena. Masochism is not so much a state of weakness as of receptivity and throbbing sensitivity. It opens us to ourselves and to the outside world. Masochism is the indispensable condition of submitting fully to an experience, encompassing realms of sex, religion, relationship, and death. It brings an arousal, an awakening, throws an odd twist into 'ordinary' or 'normal' experience. Masochism may become, with careful attention and radical curiosity, an encounter with the inevitability of one's essential character—which, as Heraclitus tells us, is Fate.

CHAPTER 7

The Fateful Move in Masochism

> *He pressed his cheek*
> *On rainwashed streets*
> *And he wept into his gin*
> *Reincarnation*
> *And he came back as himself again. . . .*
>
> PHOEBE SNOW, "It Must Be Sunday"

> *And you can cry*
> *You can lie*
> *For all the good it'll do you*
> *You can die*
> *But when it's done*
> *And the police come, and they lay you*
>   *down for dead*
> *Just remember what I said.*
>
> PAUL SIMON, "Everything Put
>   Together Falls Apart"

Character is fate, said Heraclitus; the character of masochism becomes the fate of the masochist. The gods are our portion, and to call them gods, rather than genetic dispositions or psychological mechanisms, is to speak of Fate rather than fatalism.

If character is fate, then whatever we are is fatal; it carries us to our deaths. To come to terms with one's fate entails not so much a fingertip 'getting-in-touch,' but a bone-crushing 'coming-to-grips.'

One of my analysands, a quiet, incisively intelligent, highly literate thirty-year-old woman, confessed after ten months of analysis that her *real* reason for coming into therapy was her "masochistic fantasies." Her disgust at herself and her assumption that I would be equally disgusted hung as heavy, as palpable, as curtains between us. She had exposed the root 'sickness.' Desperate with a peculiarly masochistic courage, she was doggedly and poignantly determined to get into it, under it, over it. Her style, like her content, was typically, humanly masochistic. She swung back and forth between refined poise and shattering loss of composure, humiliated submission and fist-shaking protest. Revolving in an eros of disgust and fascination, pleasure and pain, pride and suffering, she moved deeper and deeper into the fantasies.

From the moment she admitted her *real* motive for starting analysis, she was aware—sometimes frighteningly so—that she was bound to go through with it. She felt, to use her phrase, ''an imminent inevitability.'' Pressed, pushed, pulled into a welter of masochistic images, she became more and more the moved subject rather than the motivating object. Some fateful necessity was brought to bear on the therapeutic work; she had come up against her fate in the images of her masochism. This confrontation, when it pierces the heart and the matter, creates a 'third thing,' beyond the realities of analyst and analysand. It necessitates an effort of promethean proportions.

The fantasies were primarily sexual, and at the outset she felt them, above all, to be punishments. The complex was 'pathological,' sick suffering, and she was guilty of it. She felt being a masochist was punishment, deserved punishment, yet at the same time she insisted that she did not deserve to be punished so severely. Caught in a vicious cycle, she had no way out. Like Ixion on his wheel of misfortune, she felt bound to revolve endlessly—no resolution, no dissolution, no solution. It became imperative for her to see that the chains of Necessity which held her fast were also the unbreakable threads of Fate, woven into her and weaving her life patterns.

Plato says that all souls entering the world pass under the throne of Ananke (the goddess of Necessity). In Greek myth, the three goddesses of Fate, in conjunction with the working of Necessity, determine one's entrance. Fate becomes one's necessity, and necessity becomes one's fate.

Jung suggested that necessity becomes fate when the question of meaning arises.[1] It is this, he says, which transforms instinctual necessity into religious Fate. But even before the religious question of meaning or value has arisen, there is still no real separation between fate and necessity. Though distinguishable conceptually, they are inseparable in their operations. Just as the Fates are present at every birth, so every soul passes under Ananke's throne when it comes into the world. They are simultaneous presences, and the 'must' of Necessity is indistinguishable from the 'must' of Fate.

The goddess Ananke exacts perhaps her heaviest toll in and through our bodies. Her emblems—the collar, the bracelet, the belt and other accoutrements which bind and constrict—encircle our necks, limbs, wrists, publicly declaring that Necessity possesses and binds our bodies. Our bodies seem to have their own necessities and fate, which enact themselves beyond our full, or even sometimes partial, consciousness. We blink, twitch, pulsate, breathe, heal, itch, ache, orgasm, sleep, conceive, give birth, grow, and die, hardly knowing how or why. In our pride of consciousness and control, we seem incomprehensibly bound by our bodies' autonomous, and sometimes unpleasant, responses. We may suddenly—slowly—pass out, feel nauseated, bleed, go numb, blind, deaf, dumb; we may starve, become injured or diseased, go crazy, cry, laugh, hiccup, or sneeze.

Our bodies are perhaps the most solid part of our human existence, yet we recognize their necessity mostly when they malfunction. Nothing brings home our submission to our bodies better than their illnesses. Teeth, jaws, throats, glands, stomachs, bowels must perform exactly and in unison, or we are miserable—hungry, full, nauseated, pained, constipated, skinny, obese. Ananke presides commonly, inescapably, in the dining room and bathroom. Every day we are subjected to the elemental body functions of eating, urinating, and defecating. The more we escape into the disembodied dignities of the day, the more our night-soul experiences image indignities. We flush with shame when we submit to the telling of dreams like this: "I had to go to the toilet but everybody was watching and there was shit all over the floor. . . ."

Both physical and psychic Necessity belong, naturally, to all human beings, as we belong to her. Yet masochists may bear a special and especially onerous relationship to Ananke; the leather and metal collars, the chains, ropes, handcuffs, scarves, necklaces, and belts of bondage fantasies are Ananke's own emblems. These are the images of inescapability. "Necessary" means there is no choice, no escape. Its synonyms bind one to the stringency of its meaning: "inevitable," "unavoidable," "obligatory," "compulsory," "mandatory," "constraining." These are the words that bind. One can, perhaps, make adjustments around a bondage, a necessity, but one cannot get out of it.

Bodily existence binds us, mires us, in puritanical and materialistic bogs. Yet despite the pain and shame, bodily functions also bring us our greatest pleasures and delights—eating, drinking, dancing, making love, bathing, etc. So it is through the body that Necessity herself becomes a paradox: we must both desire and abhor her bonds.

Under the constraint of Ananke, we experience the pain and pleasure of necessary achievement. When Greek athletes and poets were given the laurel wreath in ancient times, it both signified an honor and bespoke a necessity: the poet *had* to write poems, the athlete *had* to do athletics, the musician *had* to make music. The laurel wreath bound, encircled, and impressed upon its wearers their natures, their fates. It was a symbol which both impressed and oppressed.

We are bound by the limits set by Fate, which is character. To transgress one's boundaries, to go beyond one's limits, is hubris, which in Greek means "beyond the allotted portion."[2] In one sense, we push back our allotted portions when we achieve goals. Achievement has that double sense of realizing one's potential, yet at the same time, pushing back one's boundaries. Discovering one's allotted portion is a lifelong and fate-filled task. One must follow inner, not outer, signposts. Submitting to one's fate is no guarantee of reward or recognition from others. It does entail self-recognition, as both its process and reward.

Prometheus knew that his fate was to transgress his boundaries, to go beyond his limits and be punished. He finally bowed to his fate of suffering for his fateful transgression. It is fitting that Prometheus was the first to bend and wear the laurel wreath, for he characterizes that achievement/submission paradox which bound him to both Ananke and Zeus. He wore an iron ring as sign of his subjection to Zeus, symbolic testimony that he had suffered titanic excesses, depths and heights, the pride and humiliation and meaning of his fate.

Probably the last thing masochism appears aimed at, in its extremity, is balance. Yet, in keeping with its paradoxical and self-tortured nature, masochism does provide a balance. Against the everyday extremity of ego and hero domination, masochism offers an extremity of soul-filled submission. It offsets the energetic bootstrap philosophy with the lowly standpoint of worn-down sandals, or goes meekly, if not reverentially, barefoot. Masochism is a mode of psychic survival. It works against the promethean fantasy which would lead to ruin. The ego is fatally prone to the hubris of promethean self-sufficiency, that illusion that one can take or steal or have what one will from the gods. When blinded by hubris and the glorious feelings it produces, the ego personality cannot see the deeper, fatal flaw: that part of its very nature is a priori lacking fire.

Once it has stolen fire—power, consciousness, life-force—the ego takes it over, calls it a possession by *right*. Life, consciousness become the spoils of war. They are no longer gifts, and we no longer acknowledge a giver. But to feel oneself reduced, exposed, and chained is to accept oneself at the mercy of the gods. This recognition is a necessary precondition for submission to one's fate.

*

Re-enter the young woman analysand with the simultaneous repulsion and attraction for her masochistic fantasies. Her daydreams and nightmares were filled with erotically seductive and unutterably horrid images of whips, handcuffs, belts, knives, rats, urine, blood, pygmies, passing out, silence. . . . Her fate was sealed in intolerable images. Those archetypes and images apportioned to us form and inform us in dreams and memories and reflections. They make our character; and as Heraclitus reminded us, character is fate. "Perhaps," wrote Jung, "the eternal images are what men mean by Fate."[3]

Like Prometheus, this woman was required to bow to Fate rather than punishment in order to be freed. This is a critical change, for it moves her masochistic inclinations from the sphere of ego, which calls down guilt and punishment for misdeeds, to the archetypal realm, which resonates with the eternal dilemma of human suffering and divine mystery. It is a religious move to bless the tie that binds. It changes her masochism from a meaningless secular psychopathology to her soul's quest and question concerning the meaning of suffering. To love one's fate is to suffer it. To suffer necessity willingly, and with love, is preeminently a religious task.

Exit Scene: This analysand exits with a fateful calm, like an initiate leaving the chamber of Dionysus in Pompeii. She takes her leave with a timeless melancholy, poised between promethean peaks and dionysian depths. Perversions, humiliations, pleasures, mortifications, martyrdoms, mountains, myriad madnesses will continue to visit her, their familiar characters reaching to embrace her. She recognizes these characters—sees that they are her character; they are her fate. As she moves offstage, she is bowed with a grounded persistence, bound in a faith which entails a realization of her necessities. The eyes of shame have seen a vision of fate; she can *exit seen*.

CHAPTER 8

Masochistic Exhibitionism: A Command Performance

> *Life's but a walking shadow, a poor player,*
> *That struts and frets his hour upon the stage,*
> *And then is heard no more; it is a tale*
> *Told by an idiot, full of sound and fury,*
> *Signifying nothing.*
>
> SHAKESPEARE, *Macbeth*

> *I strut and fret my hour*
> *Upon the stage*
> *The hour is up*
> *I have to run and hide my rage....*
>
> *And I wish I was a lover*
> *I wouldn't need my costumes*
> *And pretend....*
>
> PHOEBE SNOW, "Harpo's Blues"

•

I am lying naked in a public square, in the midst of other naked men. In the center of this quarantine camp of love, a provocatively beautiful woman, clothed in tawdry theatrical finery, is standing on an absurd scaffolding of beams and girders, like a target riddled by a thousand feverish gazes. Slowly she lifts her skirts until her belly is bare and then, with a negligent hand, she caresses the most secret recesses of her body; her face freezes in a mask of indifference; and her vague, inexpressible smile sends me spinning into an abyss.[1]

Throughout the play, the masochist, like Dionysus, wears a mask. In the theater province of Dionysus, the masochist reveals that he is not only a spineless, passive creature of misfortune, but also a forceful actor. He must act, and loves to act, and hates to act. So great is his inner torment that it must hide behind curtains and burst forth onto center stage.

On the one hand, exhibitionism attempts to activate, deepen, and intensify masochistic experience, making it real, felt, important. On the other hand, exhibitionism attempts to deny masochistic experience, reducing it to amateur charades, pushing it into the theater of the absurd. In the contradictory and paradoxical phenomenon of exhibitionism, the roles of masochist and martyr interchange in the same actor, their distinctions nearly obliterated in the spotlight's glare.

Known to psychiatry as masochistic exhibitionism, the masochist's theater is confused and confusing. The scripts are repetitious, the plots unbelievable and tormented, the endings as taxing and predictable as death itself. The self-effacing characterization, the drawn-out suffering, the shameful attitude never quite come off. No wonder then that the audience is hostile, the reviews humiliating, the masochist more masochized than ever. One can perhaps feel with the masochist a certain perverse admiration for his striking unsuccess. All of us are occasionally on some sort of stage and have to perform, even if only in the dentist's chair or at the grocery store. And whether we seek it or not, we all sometimes play the fool and learn to smile, grin and bear it, and make the most of the least. For the masochist, exhibitionism is a chance not only to perform, but to get his name up in lights. Yet actor and audience agree: exhibitionism is a dis-play which, to preserve aesthetics, ought never to have been produced. But it becomes the longest running hit-me show in town.

We all know people who hold up, exhibit, even flaunt, their emotional hurts. It is the same impulse, in adults as well as children, that prompts them to exhibit their physical wounds and scars. Masochistic exhibitionists wound easily and often. They are so oversensitized to psychic pain, so undeniably prepared for injury and rejection, that their stricken selves cry out for the final, get-it-over-with blow. But it is never over. Playing to an impossible turmoil of ambivalent feelings—in both themselves and us—they seem to be trying to dissolve and disappear at the same time that they loudly demand attention.

Psychology has linked masochism with narcissism at least partly because of its exhibitionist tendency: self-hate is linked with self-love through self-expression. Exhibitionism is then an autoerotic orgy, a self-indulgence. But we must see deeply into the exhibitionist phenomenon, into what is actually being revealed and concealed within the exhibit.

The patron god of masochism, Dionysus, wears a smiling mask. As long as we see only the smiling aspect of the mask, we must think of masochism as false pain, a histrionic—not tragic or dramatic—suffering. But as in any drama, the audience does not always recognize what it is seeing. And the masochist himself does not always know he is acting. After all, in the front of the mask, one sees a 'real' face, and behind it, one cannot see the mask at all.

The masochistic exhibitionist wears a mask of paradox. Most often, it is the revealed *ex*hibition of humiliation and pain; yet simultaneously, it is an attempted *in*hibition of pleasure. The mask is a true face, revealing an aspect of the pain and/or pleasure of a masochistic moment. The mask is the fixed, unchanging face of intolerable extremity.

But, like the god behind it, the mask also presents an illusion. Behind its strained smile hides another true face, concealing something equally alive, perhaps even more immediate to the masochist. Nietzsche said, "Every profound spirit needs a mask."[2] Once something is shown, it enters time and space, and a profundity is lost. During the exhibition, the masochist loses his sense of interiority, of the depth and privacy of his inner drama. He feels a coldness, a death of mortification, exposed to the icy glare of loveless eyes. The mask protects the wearer, as it also protects his audience. The real drama is going on behind the scene, elsewhere, backstage. The actor/masochist's pained and pleasured grimaces are hidden behind the mask's immutable smile and sightless eyes.

Perhaps because it protects, the mask also allows for the release of emotional tension. The masochist releases by thrusting forward what is happening inside. He does not have to hold all his pain in and back. Indeed, the tension and pain are often so great that they cannot be held; they must be forced outside, into the external world. It may be that the degree of exaggeration, so characteristic of masochism, is proportionate to the degree of emotional tension needing release. Subjected to the necessity of release, the masochist must, in turn, subject his world, his audience. The exhibition is, in every sense, a command performance.

This release of energy may produce an inner emptiness. As the masochist is forced to play it out on the stage, his backstage world—his inner world—empties. During an exhibitionist episode, the masochist rarely recognizes the heavy and inescapable masque that is playing *within* his own soul. If the masochist were in solid connection with his inner needs and could accept them as such, there would be no need for the drama, the exaggeration, the repetition, the mask, the forced and forceful show. But the masochist makes what is already visible painfully obvious. He apologizes before he (inevitably) offends, announces his rejection before it (inevitably) comes, slinks away before he is (inevitably) kicked out. It is because he cannot feel *enough* of his own pleasure and disgust, pain and shame that he is compelled to make his audience see *too much*.

The masochistic exhibition often displays the turmoil and fast pace of a theatrical production. In his compulsive necessity for intensity and extremity, he is bound to intensify his emotions, as a masque does. Paradoxically, for at least part of the drama, the mask becomes a wall, blocking, damming, preventing externalization. These hidden feelings then become stronger, more concentrated, like heat in a pressure cooker. The intensified feelings cannot escape, and the masochist cannot escape them. The public display becomes, at the same time, an intensified and interior experience.

Freud said that scoptophilia (the obtaining of sexual pleasure by looking at nude bodies) precedes exhibitionism, that the desire *to look at* comes before the desire *to be looked at*. These desires are inextricably bound together—the desire to look, the desire in looking, the look of desire. *Shame* stands on the other side of scoptophilia. Shame is the inhibition that prevents looking and also the intolerability of being looked at, or exposed. In masochism, exhibition and exposure are uncomfortable companions. What the masochist *exhibits* is not entirely that which he wants *exposed*. He may exhibit pain, but keep hidden the humiliation and pleasure in it. He may call attention to his failures, but not his most important, or even his most real, sins. The masochistic exhibitor tries to control, with varying degrees of success, what he wants seen. He leaps and hops onstage in a one-legged dance to make the viewer his captive audience to an illusion and a truth: is he really dancing, or is he really crippled?

The very nature of masochism, after all, demands that the masochist be crippled, a failure. But he is a successful and artistic dancer too. There is an erotic pleasure in staying within the vicious circle and in imposing it on others. Every exhibition is an erotic mating call, an attempt to attract a sadist. In this seduction, the masochist enjoys the secret shame and forbidden pleasure of being on display, caressed by everyone's eyes. If the performance is enticing enough, it lures the audience from casual observer, to voyeur, finally to sadist. In spite of the audience's being disgusted and hostile—or indeed, *because* of it—the star can end secretly applauding himself. Curtains.

Showing off, covering up, secret success and blatant unsuccess, protection, release, exposure, intensification, externalization, internalization . . . no wonder the drama is confused and confusing!

Perhaps the element most simple and apparent in masochistic exhibitionism is that face of compulsion, fixation, that necessity to reveal—and hide—one's private pain, and one's unspeakable pleasure in doing so. Whatever the style of exhibition, one factor is always present and always hidden behind the mask: self-disgust. During the exhibition, it is just the pain and self-disgust of being a masochist and an exhibitionist which can least be shown—but is most felt.

Disgust opposes shame and is a defensive move against it. Under the constant assault of so much shame, the masochist retreats toward its opposite. A colleague of mine has observed that the exhibitionist needs to make his audience disgusted in order to feel more humiliated; through others, he feels again, in crescendos of quantity and quality, just how disgusting he really is.[3] This is the vicious masochistic circle: all the world's a sadist and the masochist is always a masochist. This viciousness revolves with renewed energy every time the masochist identifies himself in terms of another's disgust.

Where the masochist and his audience are united in disgust, they are joined in a conspiracy against *aidos*, shame. Shame, Aristotle said, dwells in the eyes; but disgust turns away, without making inner eye contact, and sees only the surface, the falsity—not the true shame or the real meaning. And so disgust changes nothing.

It is not disgust, but respect, which is the antidote to too much shame. Masochists want to be respected, loved, not merely seen. But bound in their worthlessness and humiliation, arrogance and pain, they cannot deserve love. Love to the masochist is a fearful and impossible thing. In his insatiability, exaggerated attention-getting, tireless manipulation, and inability to accept love even when offered, the masochist receives pity—which invites still more disgust. This attitude protects his familiar humiliation by keeping him in his lowly state, and protects his familiar pain by keeping him on the edge of tormenting doubt about his real self-worth.

Just on the other side of defeat and deflation is the secret hope that he just might be worthy of love. "Look at me, I'm in pain" means "Love me in spite of myself." In his frenzied, unstable demand for respect, he may reveal a pathologized pride in his acting, endurance, abilities. "You'd better love me an impossible lot!" is the real meaning. It is a mangled message coming out in a strangled cry, as heart-rending and embarrassing as a clumsy clown alone in the center ring. It places a heavy burden on the observer, who is silently but desperately pressed to overcome his disgust of the exhibitionist's shameless display of raw need.

The sadist and masochist both long to strip off the mask, both revealing and releasing the masochist. The masochist desires the exhibition to become an exposure, so that he can stop the acting, take a break, be broken, get out from under the weight and rigidity of the mask/masque. He desires, he longs, he needs, to love the unlovely—himself. As long as they are caught in the compulsivity and viciousness of the circle, neither the humiliated masochist nor the disgusted audience reaches that sensitizing shame which can lead to self-reflection and self-respect.

In a way, the masochist shows nothing that we don't all have—and show too. The difference is in the staging of the exhibition and in the paradoxical desired effects on the audience. In masochism, the staging is extreme, stark, compulsive. Thus it is extremely embarrassing, extremely repellent, and extremely titillating to the onlookers. Trapped in his never-ending play, the masochistic exhibitionist has a keen sense that all the world's a stage. He often lives in a kind of theatrical dionysian frenzy, compelled to repeat performances in his relationships, fantasies, and dreams. And long after the lights have gone out, he plays it again, damned, now himself an audience of one, the catcalls echoing again and again in the theater of his memory.

The gods have many shapes.
The gods bring many things
to their accomplishment.
And what was most expected
has not been accomplished.
But god has found his way
for what no man expected.
  So ends the play.
                    EURIPIDES, *The Bacchae*

Notes

The abbreviation *CW* refers throughout these notes to *The Collected Works of C. G. Jung*, trans. R. F. C. Hull, Bollingen Series XX, vols. 1–20 (Princeton: Princeton Univ. Press, 2nd ed., 1969), paragraph nos.

An Opening

1. Ann Landers, Field Newspaper Syndicate column in the *Minneapolis Tribune*, 25 May 1980.
2. Jung, *CW* 11, §8.
3. James Hillman, *Re-Visioning Psychology* (New York: Harper & Row, 1975), p. x.
4. Jung, *CW* 6, §78.
5. Ibid., §722.
6. Hillman, p. 71.
7. Jung, *CW* 13, §75.
8. Patricia Berry, "An Approach to the Dream," *Spring 1974*, p. 62.
9. Jung defines "archetype" as both a "primordial image" (*CW* 6, §747) and as a predisposition to an image or a "possibility of representation"; he describes it by analogy to "the axial system of a crystal, which, as it were, preforms the crystalline structure in the mother liquid, although it has no material existence of its own" (*CW* 9-I, §155). Archetypes are "typical modes of apprehension" (*CW* 8, §273). Hillman describes archetypes as "the *deepest patterns of psychic functioning* [italics his], the roots of the soul governing the perspectives we have of ourselves and the world. They are the axiomatic, self-evident images to which psychic life and our theories about it ever return" (*Re-Visioning*, p. xiii).
10. Nor Hall, *The Moon and the Virgin: Reflections on the Archetypal Feminine* (New York: Harper & Row, 1980), p. 28.

Chapter 1

1. Jung defines the individuation process as "in general . . . . the process by which individual beings are formed and differentiated; in particular, it is the development of the psychological *individual* as a being distinct from the general,

132

collective psychology. Individuation, therefore, is a process of *differentiation*, having for its goal the development of the individual personality'' (*CW* 6, §757).

2. James Hillman, ''Archetypal Theory,'' in *Loose Ends* (Spring Publications, 1975), p. 176.

3. Richard von Krafft-Ebing, *Psychopathia Sexualis*, trans. Franklin S. Klaf (New York: Stein & Day, 1965), p. 86.

4. Ibid., p. 139.

5. Ibid., p. 138.

6. Ibid., p. 3.

7. Leopold von Sacher-Masoch, *Venus in Furs*, trans. Jean McNeil. The text I am using in this book is printed in its entirety as part of Gilles Deleuze, *Masochism: An Interpretation of Coldness and Cruelty* (New York: George Braziller, 1971), p. 123.

8. For a discussion of the north/south idea of psychic geography, see Hillman, *Re-Visioning Psychology* (New York: Harper & Row, 1975), pp. 219 f., 223, 260 n.116.

9. Masoch, p. 121.

10. Sigmund Freud, ''The Economic Problem in Masochism,'' vol. 2 of *Collected Papers* (New York: Basic Books, Inc., 1959), p. 266.

11. Freud, ''A Child is Being Beaten,'' op. cit., p. 184.

12. Freud, ''Economic Problem,'' p. 263.

13. Freud, ''Analysis Terminable and Interminable,'' vol. 5 of *Collected Papers*, p. 346.

14. The Penitentials, manuals which codified sins and penances, were used by confessors as guides. They were used in Christian Europe from the sixth through the eleventh centuries, after which they gradually fell into disuse. (Confession became obligatory at least once a year for all Christians in 1215, by decree of the Fourth Lateran Council.) The chief interest of the Penitentials for psychology is that they shifted the emphasis, to some degree, from an external recognition of sin to an internal one (i.e., that sin is as much a state of 'being' as of 'doing'), and thus encouraged and continued, in a Christian context, that introspection which began with St. Augustine's *Confessions*. Regardless of their rather crude codifications of the soul's diseases, they were nevertheless attempts to go to the roots of sin, and to deepen individual religious experience.

15. John T. McNeill, ''Medicine for Sin as Prescribed in the Penitentials,'' *Church History* I (1932): 14–26.

16. St. Teresa of Avila, *Spiritual Relations*, in *The Complete Works of Saint*

Teresa of Jesus, vol. 1 (New York: Sheed & Ward, 1946), p. 307.

17. Norman Cohn, *The Pursuit of the Millenium* (New York: Oxford Univ. Press, 1970), p. 128.

18. Ibid.

19. Franz Alexander and Sheldon Selesnick, *The History of Psychiatry* (New York: Harper & Row, 1966), p. 62.

20. Jung, *CW* 10, §659; see also *CW* 14, §603 and *CW* 17, §157.

21. The Greek word *pathos* means a capacity to be moved or being moved, essentially "something that happens." *Pathos* and suffering are not necessarily the same thing, but suffering may be one of the movements *(pathe)* of the soul. Cf. Hillman, *Re-Visioning*, pp. 95–99 for more on the crucifixion image and pathology. Hillman's two specific references to "sado-masochism" in these pages are, I believe, used in a more limited sense than I am using them in this book.

22. Jung, *CW* 13, §54–55.

23. Carl Schneider, *Shame, Exposure, and Privacy* (Boston: Beacon Press, 1977), p. 111.

24. Joseph Gendron, personal communication.

25. Hillman, *Re-Visioning*, p. xiv.

26. Russell Lockhart, "Cancer in Myth and Dream," *Spring 1977*, p. 21.

27. Hillman, *Loose Ends*, p. 180.

28. Adolf Guggenbühl-Craig, *Marriage: Dead or Alive* (Spring Publications, 1977), pp. 86–87.

Chapter 2

1. The shadow is Jung's term for that part of the personality which is "the sum of all personal and collective psychic elements which, because of their incompatibility with the chosen conscious attitude, are denied expression in life and therefore coalesce into a relatively autonomous 'splinter personality' with contrary tendencies in the unconscious. The shadow behaves compensatorily to consciousness; hence its effects can be positive as well as negative" (*Memories, Dreams, Reflections* [New York: Vintage Books, 1965], pp. 386–87).

2. "Closer to the Ground," lyrics by Toni Brown, Bear Brown Publishing Co., 1978.

Chapter 3

1. Patricia Berry, "The Dogma of Gender: Straight and Perverse," a paper presented at the Guild of Pastoral Psychology, Royal Society of Medicine, London, 1977.

2. Leopold von Sacher-Masoch, *Venus in Furs*, trans. Jean McNeil, in Gilles Deleuze, *Masochism: An Interpretation of Coldness and Cruelty* (New York: George Braziller, 1971), pp. 165–66.

3. Gerald and Caroline Greene, *S-M: The Last Taboo* (New York: Grove Press, Inc., 1974), p. 54.

4. Theodor Reik, *Of Love and Lust* (New York: Farrar, Straus & Cudahy, 1957), p. 233.

5. Berry, "Dogma of Gender."

6. Masoch, p. 149.

7. The term was used first by the poet Keats in a letter to his brother in 1819, but James Hillman made the idea his theme in his masterful *Re-Visioning Psychology*.

8. Mario Praz, *The Romantic Agony*, trans. Angus Davidson (London: Oxford Univ. Press, 1970), p. 31.

9. Deleuze, p. 64.

10. Referring specifically to Masoch's preoccupation with fur, coldness, and cruelty in *Venus in Furs*, and, by extension, to masochism in general, Deleuze, p. 81, says of the masochistic contract that it "generates a type of law which leads straight into ritual. The masochist is obsessed; ritualistic activity is essential to him, since it epitomizes the world of phantasy." I would question here whether the essential need for ritual activity denotes obsession in all cases as a psychopathological symptom. We all need fantasy, we all need ritual activities, to some degree or another. There is no ground for placing the masochist in a special category, as "obsessive," because he needs much the same thing all humans do. The difference may be more in how he meets this need than in what he needs.

Deleuze discusses the three types of rites in Masoch's novels—hunting, agriculture, and regeneration/rebirth—which I include here as interesting ideas. Deleuze says these three rites echo three fundamental elements of masochism: "the cold, that requires the conquest of the fur, the trophy of the hunt; the buried sentimentality and sheltered fecundity which agriculture demands, together with the strictest organization of work; and finally that very element of strictness, that cruel rigour which regeneration and rebirth demand. The co-existence and interaction of these three rites sum up the mythical complex of masochism'' (p. 81).

11. Nancy Friday, *My Secret Garden* (New York: Pocket Books, 1974), p. 124.

12. Reik, p. 216.

13. Berry, "Dogma of Gender."

14. Ibid.

15. John Fowles, *The Magus: A Revised Version* (Boston: Little, Brown & Co., 1977), p. 269.

16. Karl Kerényi, *Hermes, Guide of Souls*, trans. Murray Stein (Spring Publications, 1976), pp. 55–56.

Chapter 4

1. Thanks to James Hillman for this neologism.

2. Mundus, "Sermo XVIII," quoted in Jung, *CW* 13, §439.

3. Quoted in Christopher Ricks, *Keats and Embarrassment* (Oxford: Clarendon Press, 1974), p. 26.

4. Ibid., p. 54.

5. Hillman, *Lectures on Alchemy*, presented at the C. G. Jung Institut–Zürich, 1974.

6. Franz Kafka, "A Report to an Academy," in *The Penal Colony: Stories and Short Pieces* (New York: Schocken Books, 1961), p. 183.

7. Hillman, *Re-Visioning Psychology* (New York: Harper & Row, 1975), p. 186.

8. The dreamer had been to a seminar on "Guilt and Shame" some months prior to this dream, where she learned that *aidos* is a Greek word for "shame" with the particular sense of awe and reverence. But in the dream she did not recognize or understand the word.

Chapter 5

1. *The Random House Dictionary of the English Language*, unabridged ed. (New York: Random House, 1967).

2. Nor Hall, *The Moon and the Virgin: Reflections on the Archetypal Feminine* (New York: Harper & Row, 1980), p. 28.

Chapter 6

1. Charles Morgan, *Sparkenbroke* (New York: The Macmillan Co., 1936), p. 385.

2. E. R. Dodds, *The Greeks and the Irrational* (Berkeley: Univ. of California Press, 1968), p. 77.

3. Karen Horney, *New Ways in Psychoanalysis* (New York: W. W. Norton & Co., Inc., 1966), p. 248.

4. Richard von Krafft-Ebing, *Psychopathia Sexualis*, trans. Franklin S. Klaf (New York: Stein & Day, 1965), p. 23.

5. G. G. Coulton, *Five Centuries of Religion*, vol. II (London: Cambridge Univ. Press, 1927), p. 158.

6. Maiui's view is cited by Linda Fierz-David, *The Villa dei Misteri, Pompeii: A Psychological Essay*, trans. Gladys Phelan (Zürich: unpublished typescript, 1957).

7. Fierz-David, *Villa dei Misteri*.

8. Euripides, *The Bacchae*, trans. William Arrowsmith, in *Greek Tragedies*, vol. 3, ed. David Grene and Richmond Lattimore (Chicago: The Univ. of Chicago Press, 1960), line 113.

9. E. R. Dodds, *Euripides' Bacchae* (Oxford: Clarendon Press, 1960), p. 82.

10. Russell Lockhart, "Eros in Language, Myth, and Dream," *Quadrant*, Summer 1978, p. 44.

11. W. F. Otto, *Dionysus: Myth and Cult* (Dallas: Spring Publications, 1981), p. 180.

12. Dodds, "Maenadism in *The Bacchae*," *Harvard Theological Review*, July 1940, p. 165.

13. Otto, pp. 140–41.

14. James Hillman, *Myth of Analysis* (Evanston: Northwestern Univ. Press, 1972), p. 146.

15. Leopold von Sacher-Masoch, *Venus in Furs*, trans. Jean McNeil, in Gilles Deleuze, *Masochism: An Interpretation of Coldness and Cruelty* (New York: George Braziller, 1971), p. 140.

16. Krafft-Ebing, p. 130.

17. Otto, p. 179.

18. Nancy Friday, *My Secret Garden* (New York: Pocket Books, 1974), p. 130.

19. Arthur Adamov, *L'Aveu (Confession)* (Paris, 1946), quoted in *Erotic Fantasies: A Study of the Sexual Imagination*, ed. Phyllis and Eberhard Kronhausen (New York: Bell Publishing Co., 1969), p. 221.

20. C. Kerényi, *Dionysos*, trans. Ralph Manheim, vol. 2 of Bollingen Series LXV, *Archetypal Images in Greek Religion* (Princeton: Princeton Univ. Press, 1976), p. 359.

21. Otto, p. 143.

22. Euripides, *The Bacchae*, lines 725–28.

23. Jung, *CW* 6, §227.

Chapter 7

1. Jung, *CW* 17, §299 ff.

2. The word also literally means "to run riot."

3. Jung, *CW* 7, §183.

Chapter 8

1. Arthur Adamov, *L'Aveu (Confession)* (Paris, 1946), quoted in *Erotic Fantasies: A Study of the Sexual Imagination*, ed. Phyllis and Eberhard Kronhausen (New York: Bell Publishing Co., 1969), p. 221.

2. Friedrich Nietzsche, *Beyond Good and Evil* (New York: The Modern Library, 1954), p. 426.

3. Mary Lynn Kittelson, personal communication.

Pathology Revisioned

THE FAR SIDE OF MADNESS   *John Weir Perry*
First published in 1974, this pioneering work reframes acute psychotic
episodes in the context of visionary experience and describes the
resulting innovative methods of handling them. Through Dr. Perry's
extensive experience with patients on hospital wards, he came to see
the psychotic episode as "a renewal process." (177 pp.)

ON PARANOIA   *James Hillman*
How can we distinguish religious revelation from pathological delusion, since both are "attempts to adjust to the unseen order"? Hillman
studies in careful detail three cases, finding interwoven sexual and
religious images. The argument shows that the absoluteness of revelation always has a paranoid effect and that paranoia always implicates
a vision of truth. (56 pp.)

DARK EROS
The Imagination of Sadism   *Thomas Moore*
From thousands of pages of the Marquis de Sade's fiction, Moore
crystallizes the "Sadeian imagination," revealing the hidden soul values
in the shocking phenomena of sado-masochism. He connects Sade's
themes of isolation, bondage, violence, black humor, and naive in-
nocence with patterns in education, therapy, marriage, and religion.
(190 pp.)

INCEST AND HUMAN LOVE   *Robert Stein*
Explores the Incest Taboo for a vision of therapy that can heal the
love/sex dichotomy. Chapters on Eros and its transformation, on
Phallos in male and female psychology, on the incest wound in the
archetypal family situation together provide an uncompromising,
sincerely felt challenge to conventional ego psychology, Jungian con-
servatism, Freudian reductionism, and to every method that veers away
from the animal level of the human soul. This third edition includes
a new introduction. (xxi, 200 pp.)

Spring Publications, Inc. • *P.O. Box 222069* • *Dallas, Texas 75222*

Books of Permanent Jungian Interest

WOMEN'S DIONYSIAN INITIATION   *Linda Fierz-David*
Rare Pompeiian fresco art depicting an initiation ceremony for women
in a series of ten exquisite scenes provides the basic material for the
author's psychological analysis. We feel the events of extraordinary
life lived in the company of Dionysos from Ariadne's point of view.
These ancient mysteries once enacted collectively continue today, according to M. Esther Harding's introduction, in "the secret recesses
of the heart." Color plates. (149 pp.)

A CELTIC QUEST   *John Layard*
This classic Welsh tale of heroic youth in search of soul finds a master
equal to its riddles in John Layard, Oxford anthropologist and Jungian
analyst. The quest proceeds as a boar hunt, encountering giants and
dwarfs, bitch-dogs, helpful ants, the Witch Hag, until the soul is won.
The standard psychological interpretation of Celtic legend includes
appendices, scholarly apparatus, index. (264 pp.)

THE LOGOS OF THE SOUL   *Evangelos Christou*
Christou pushes the languages of science, philosophy, and art to their
limit, demonstrating that only psychological reality creates the experience that is at the same time its object of study. One must be
prepared for the conclusions of such insight: all psychology is
psychotherapy; manifestation, not adaptation, measures therapeutic
effectiveness; therapy with another is always self therapy; self-therapy
is inextricably world therapy. (iv, 104 pp.)

THE SELF IN PSYCHOTIC PROCESS   *John Weir Perry*
The case of the young housewife diagnosed catatonic schizophrenic
demonstrates the interpenetration of collective symbols and individual
processes as they come to light in "breakdown" (Part One) and ex-
tends knowledge of the psyche by elucidating symbols of the Self (Part
Two). This second edition includes a new preface by Dr. Perry, together
with the original Foreword by C. G. Jung, scholarly apparatus, illustrations, and index. (xv, 184 pp.)

Spring Publications, Inc. • *P.O. Box 222069* • *Dallas, Texas 75222*